BULLETIN BOARD BRAINSTORMS

HOLIDAY HAPPENINGS

WRITTEN BY SUSANNE GLOVER & GEORGEANN GREWE
ILLUSTRATED BY BEV ARMSTRONG

The Learning Works

Printed in the United States of America.

TO THE TEACHER

Holiday Happenings contains creative ideas for seasonal bulletin board displays and related student art projects and activities. Three separate board layouts are presented for each month, September through May. These seasonal and thematic boards are designed not only to be decorative but also to become suitable backdrops for the effective display of student work. Patterns and easy-to-follow instructions enable children to create artwork that readily becomes an integral part of each bulletin board display.

For each display, there is a detailed drawing, a list of materials needed, a paragraph of simple assembly instructions, and a brief description of related activities.

Suggestions are supplied for assembling each bulletin board display, and patterns and illustrated step-by-step instructions are provided for each student art project. Needed materials have been kept to a minimum and are listed. For most displays and projects, they include butcher, construction, crepe, and tissue paper in a variety of colors. In addition, some projects require tagboard, paper bags, empty cardboard tubes, cotton balls, popsicle sticks, tongue depressors, twist ties or florist's wire, foil, ribbon, yarn, glitter, pipe cleaners, or paper plates. Also needed, but not listed, are standard art supplies, such as pencils, rulers, scissors, paste or glue, crayons or marking pens, tempera paints and brushes, paper punch, stapler, and staples.

Related activities are designed to help you extend bulletin board themes into other content areas. They include math and language arts skill sheets and word search puzzles, and offer students opportunities for independent research and additional creative involvement.

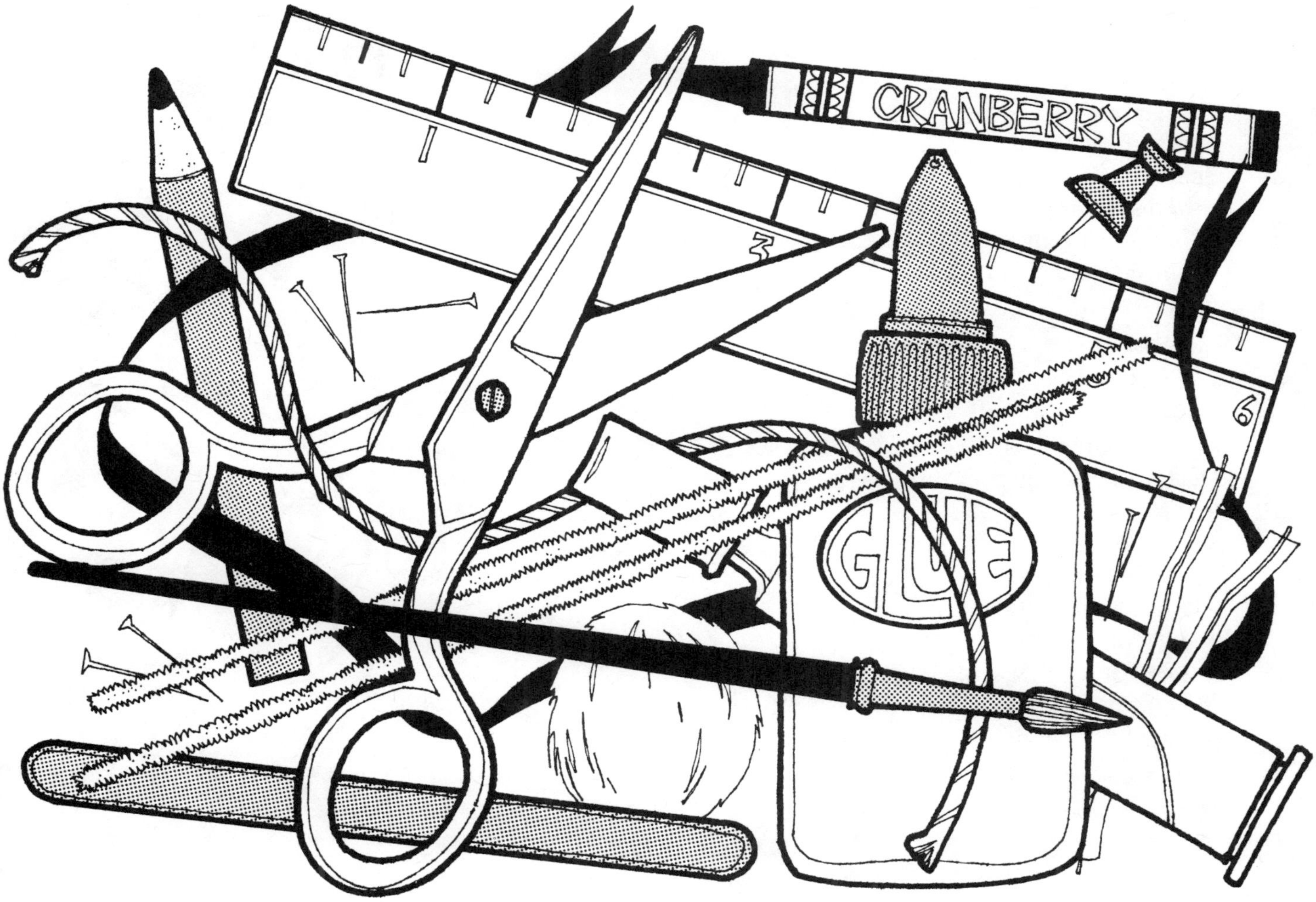

CONTENTS

RULER, PAPER, SCISSORS, PEN, SCHOOL IS STARTING ONCE AGAIN

Materials

red background
black-and-white striped border
drawing paper for rebus pictures
white letters for written parts of rebus words
large manila or clasp envelope to hold pictures and letters
large manila or clasp envelope to hold activity sheets on pages 7, 8, and 9

Instructions

Put up the background and add the border. Cut white letters, then copy and cut out the ruler, paper, scissors, pen, school, star, and number shapes. Staple letters and pictures to the board to make a rebus. Add envelopes to hold spare letters or pictures and activity sheets. By means of the photocopy or thermofax process, make copies of the activity sheets on pages 7, 8, and 9. Hand one copy of each sheet to each member of your class as you prepare to do the activities described below.

Activities

- **The Long Ride**—Ask each student to cut out the pictures on page 8 and paste one of them in each box on page 7 to create a rebus.
- **Rebus Writing**—Help students become better acquainted with rebus writing by encouraging them to replace the words on this page with pictures.

Name ______________________

THE LONG RIDE

A **rebus** is a statement, riddle, or story in which pictures or symbols take the place of some or all of the words. Cut apart the pictures on page 8. Paste one picture in each box in this story to create a rebus.

On the day of , I was waiting beside the road for my to pick me up. I was carrying my new book bag with my , , , and inside it. In my other hand, I was holding my . I couldn't wait to see my friends again!

Soon I saw the coming down my road. It stopped, and I got on. The road was bumpy, and I hadn't had time to eat breakfast. The ride to seemed so long. I guess that I was just too excited. I felt dizzy, so I leaned over. When I looked up, the had stopped in front of the , and my teacher was standing at the door ringing the for class to t

Name ______________________________

PICTURES FOR THE LONG RIDE

A **rebus** is a statement, riddle, or story in which pictures or symbols take the place of some or all of the words. Cut apart the pictures below. Paste one picture in each box on page 7 to create a rebus.

Name ________________________________

REBUS WRITING

Rewrite the lines below using pictures to illustrate as many words or parts of words as you can.

1. A sandwich and cookies in my lunch
   Plus many green grapes in a bunch.

2. Spelling, math, science, reading . . .
   My favorite time is when I'm eating!

3. The bell has rung.
   Please find your seat.
   Head your papers
   Nice and neat.

HEADING FOR (YOUR SCHOOL)

Materials

yellow background
large football player dressed in school colors
black-and-white striped letters spelling **Heading for (the name of your school)**
construction, photocopy, or ditto paper for individual helmets (to be made by students)

Instructions

Put up the background and add the player and letters. Using the photocopy or thermofax process, make copies of the football helmet (page 11), admission ticket (page 12), and blank ticket (page 13). Hand one copy of each sheet to each member of your class as you prepare to do the activities described below.

Activities

- **Football Helmet**—Ask each student to decorate a helmet using both the school colors and official insignia. If your school does not have either special colors or an insignia, suggest students use original color combinations and create insignia. Urge students to consider and then list their goals for the school year.
- **Admission Ticket**—Allow time for students to supply the information called for on the ticket.
- **Blank Ticket**—Have each student use this sheet to write a creative story about the travels of a ticket.

Name ____________________

FOOTBALL HELMET

Carefully avoiding the lines and the circle, decorate this helmet using your school colors. Next, either design or copy your school insignia within the circle. Then, list your goals for the school year on the lines. When you have finished, cut out your helmet and add it to the class display.

Name ______________________

ADMISSION TICKET

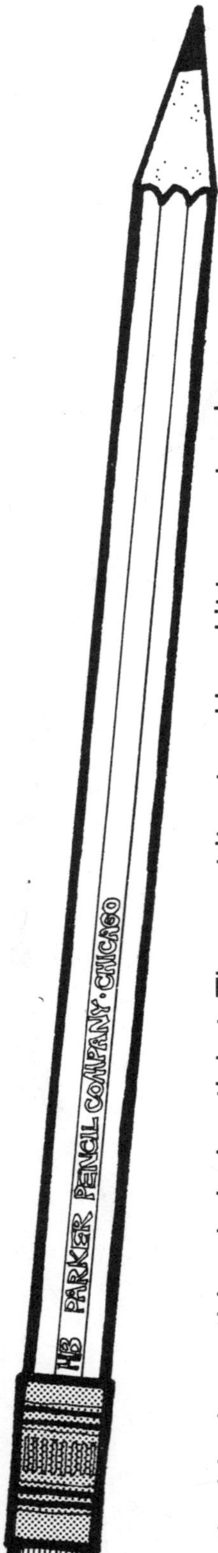

Fill in the blanks on this admission ticket. Then, cut it out and hand it to your teacher.

ADMIT ONE

★★★★★★★★★★

Row______ **Seat**______

NAME: ______________________

SCHOOL: ______________________

TELEPHONE NUMBER: ______________________

TEACHER: ______________________

BIRTHDAY: ______________________

AGE: ______________________

FAVORITE SUBJECT: ______________________

LEAST LIKED SUBJECT ______________________

BEST FRIEND IN THIS CLASS: ______________________

HOBBIES: ______________________

____

Name ____________________

BLANK TICKET

Pretend that you are a ticket. In a story, describe what kind of ticket you are, where you were bought, how much you cost, where you have been, where you are going, and what interesting experiences you've had along the way.

A HANDSOME CLASS

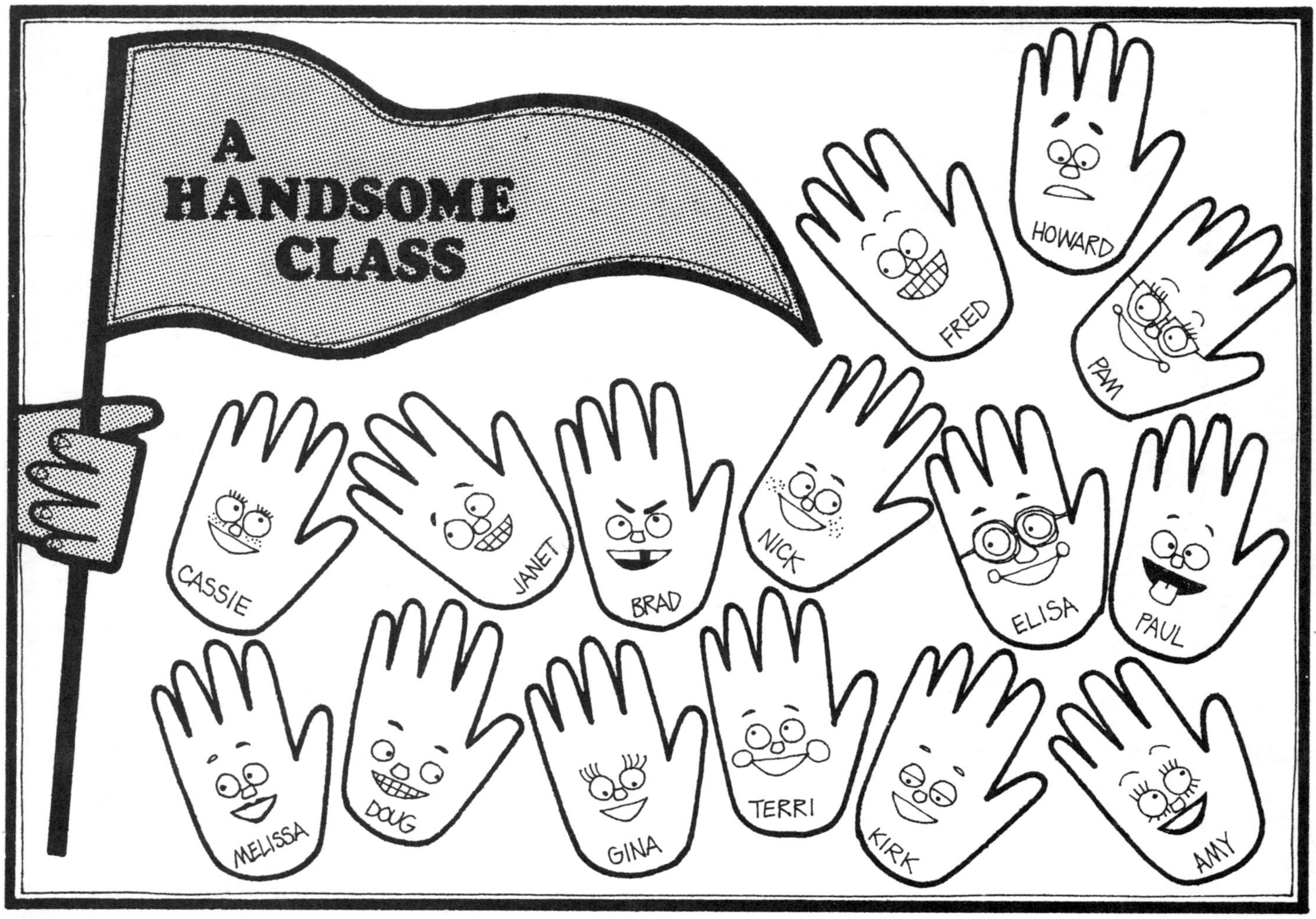

Materials

yellow background
black flagpole, red pennant, and pink or flesh-toned hand grasping flagpole
white letters on flag spelling **A Handsome Class**
pastel or white construction paper for hands (to be made by students)

Instructions

Put up the background and add the flagpole, pennant, and letters. Using the photocopy or thermofax process, make several copies of page 15. Cut out the hand pattern pieces. Mount them on tagboard or other stiff paper, or place them on tagboard, trace around them, and cut them out to make additional pattern pieces for class members to use.

Activities

- **Hand Pattern**—Have each child use the pattern provided to make a personalized hand for display on the bulletin board.
- **Personal Inventory Hand**—Ask each child to supply the needed information and then cut out the hand. Display each child's inventory hand beside his personalized one on the board, or have children glue inventory hands to the backs of personalized ones.

HAND PATTERN

Make available hand patterns and construction paper. Ask each child to make a personalized hand. Suggest that children not only use pattern pieces to add facial features, but also that they add distinctive touches, such as freckles, eyebrows, eyelashes, and glasses. You may wish to have them curl the fingers forward to form hair. After they have finished, remind them to print their names at the bottom. Then, post the hands on the board.

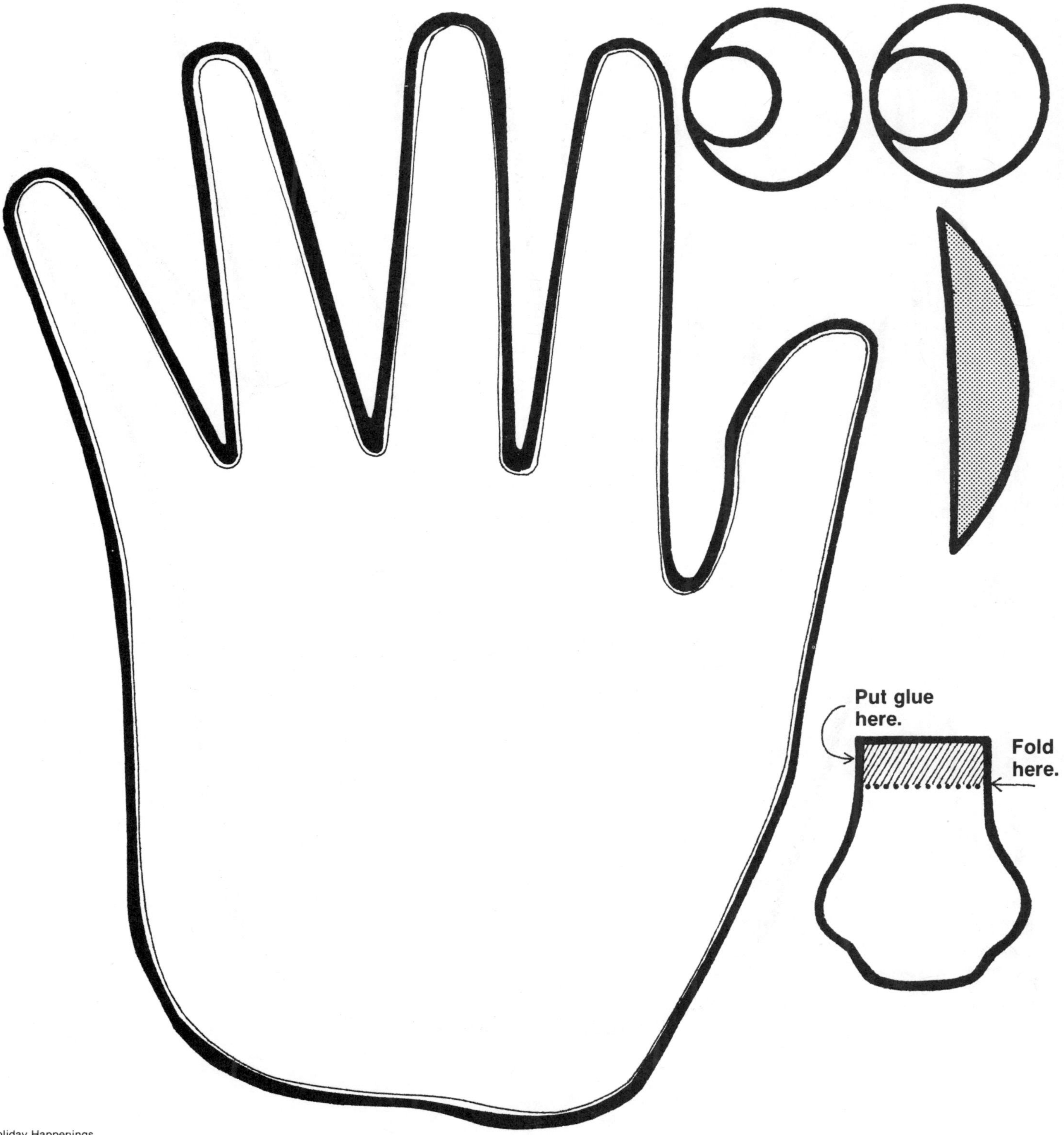

Name ______________________________

PERSONAL INVENTORY HAND

Fill in the blanks on hand. Then, cut it out and hand it to your teacher.

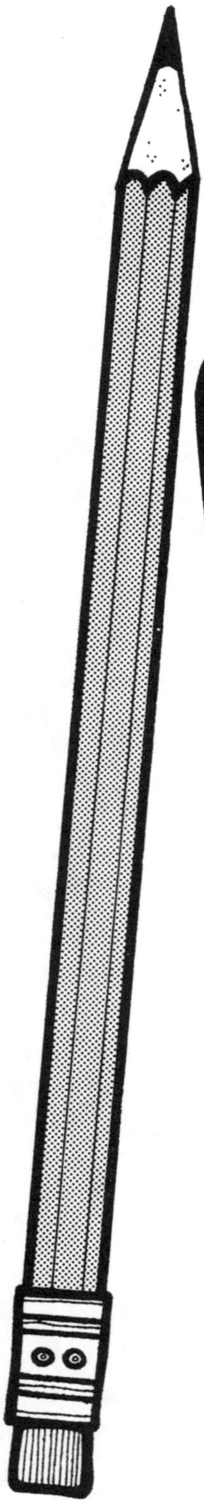

My Name: ____________________________

My Age: ______________________________

Number of Brothers I Have: _________

Number of Sisters I Have: __________

My Birthday: _________________________

My Favorite Color: __________________

My Favorite Food: ___________________

My Pets: _____________________________

____

____

My Hobbies: __________________________

____

____

IT'S OWL-OWEEN!

Materials

yellow background
brown or orange letters and punctuation marks spelling **It's Owl-oween!**
large brown butcher paper tree trunk with at least one limb and a black construction paper hole
large construction paper owl to live in the hole
green construction paper for tree leaves
one small, brown paper bag for each child in the class
owl puppet activity sheet (page 18)

Instructions

Put up the background and add the tree, large owl, leaves, and letters. By means of the photocopy or thermofax process, make copies of the owl puppet on page 18, the Who's Wise subtraction review sheet on page 19, and the Give a Hoot research sheet on page 20 to use when doing the activities described below.

Activities

- **Owl Puppet**—Have children make owl puppets using the parts shown on page 18.
- **Who's Wise?**—Allow time for children to complete this subtraction review sheet.
- **Owl Report**—Instruct children to choose a specific species of owl to study and report on using the Give a Hoot activity sheet on page 20.

Name ____________________

OWL PUPPET

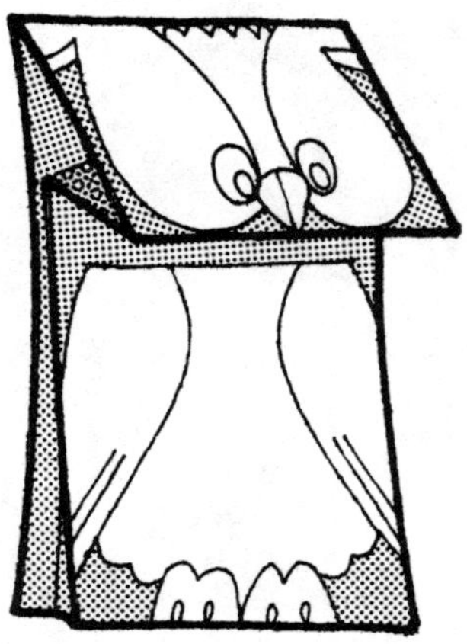

Color the owl. Cut out the head and body. Glue each piece to a paper bag as shown.

Name ______________________

WHO'S WISE?

				1.	23 -11	2.	44 -32
3.	76 -28	4.	84 -57	5.	63 -26	6.	81 -59
7.	92 -44	8.	65 -26	9.	96 -47	10.	35 -17
11.	134 - 69	12.	228 - 49	13.	762 - 98	14.	531 - 62
15.	206 -156	16.	837 -428	17.	531 -275	18.	943 -174
19.	7324 -3588	20.	5673 -4294	21.	8642 -3795	22.	3667 -1878

Name ____________________

GIVE A HOOT

Visit your local library to read about an interesting type of owl. On the branch below, draw and color a picture of the owl that you chose.

On the lines below, list five fascinating facts about your type of owl.

1. ____________________
2. ____________________
3. ____________________
4. ____________________
5. ____________________

Find a poem about an owl. Using your neatest handwriting, copy it in the space provided. Or write a poem of your own!

____

____
____
____
____
____
____
____
____
____

WITCHES HAVE CLASS

Materials

orange background
large yellow crescent moon with profile and oblong black-and-white eye
black letters spelling **Witches Have Class**
long brown construction paper broom. (For a three-dimensional effect, use either a lightweight broom or a cylindrical object with butcher paper strips for broomstraw.)
witch pattern sheets (pages 22 and 23)
at least two cotton balls for each student

Instructions

Put up the background. Add the moon, broom, and letters. By means of the photocopy or thermofax process, make copies of the witch pattern on pages 22 and 23 and the homophone activity sheet on page 24 to use when you do the activities described below.

Activities

- **Witches**—Help children assemble witches using the pattern pieces and instructions on pages 22 and 23.
- **Homophone Activity Sheet**—Complement the witch art lesson with the Witch Weigh/Which Way activity sheet on page 24.

Name ______________________________

WITCH PATTERN

1. Cut out all of the pattern pieces on pages 22 and 23.

2. 

Roll paper and glue or staple edges of the body to make a cone.

3. 

Glue on the face.
Glue on cotton balls for hair, leaving the point free.

4. 

Glue on the broom.

5. 

Glue one arm on each side.

6. 

Slide the hat brim down over the point.

7. Add your finished witch to the display.

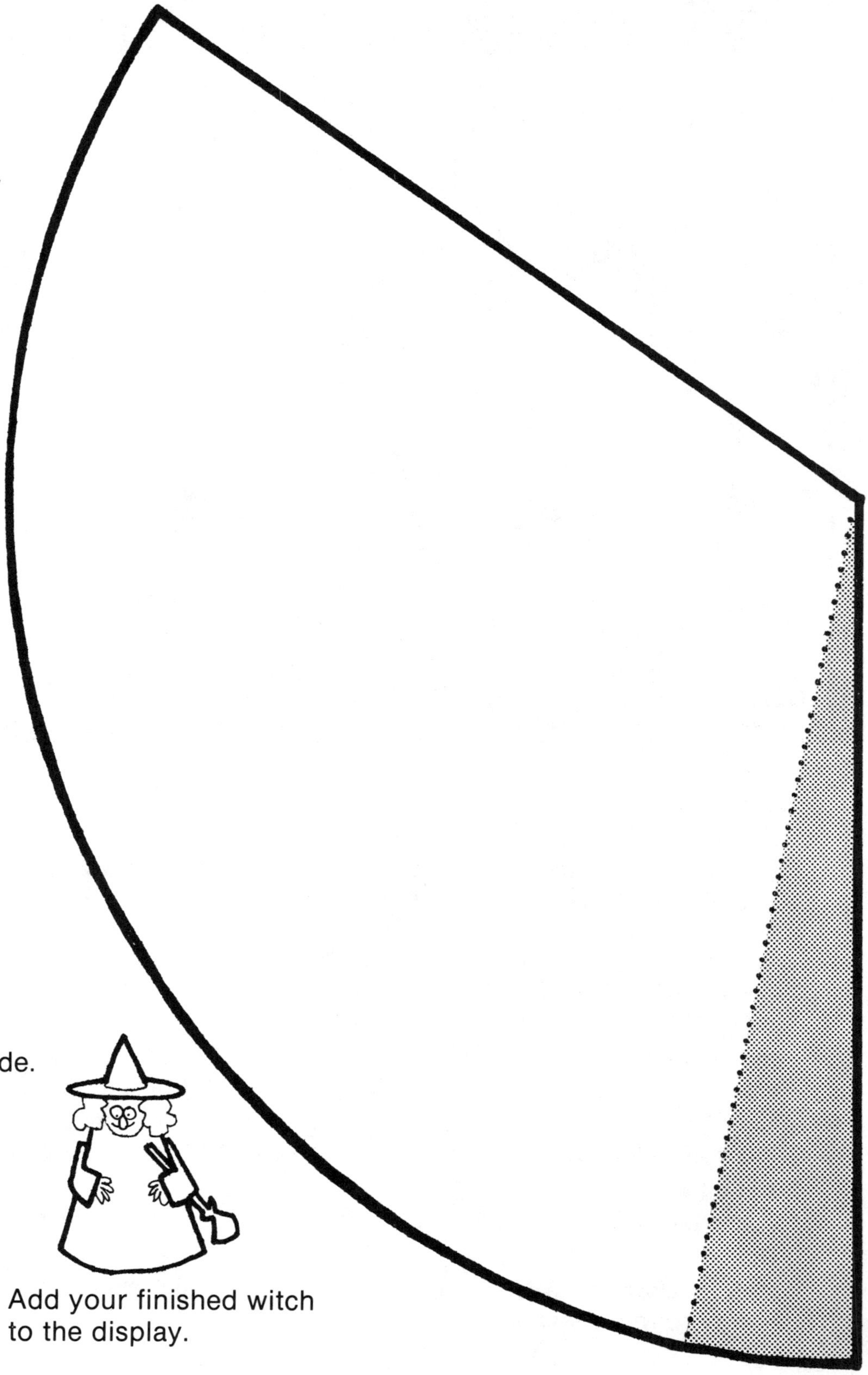

Name ______________________________

WITCH PATTERN
(continued)

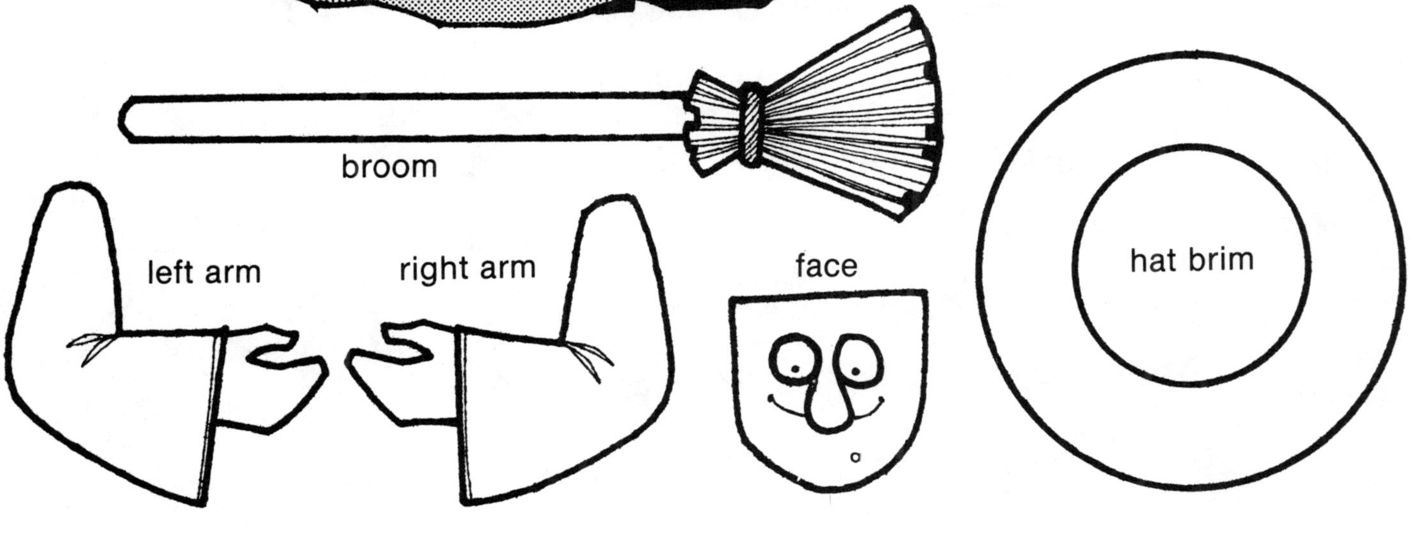

Name ______________________________

WITCH WEIGH/WHICH WAY?

A **homophone** is a word that sounds exactly like another word but has a different spelling and/or a different meaning. Circle the correct homophone in each of the sentences below.

1. (Eye, I) walked (buy, by) your house on my way home.
2. The (witch, which) could (knot, not) stay on her broom.
3. (Hour, Our) dog stepped on a (be, bee).
4. I (one, won) the game with (to, two) homeruns.
5. Tom lost his (blew, blue) jacket in the (hi, high) grass.
6. (We, Wee) should not (waist, waste) food.
7. The (bare, bear) sat in the (we,wee) chair.
8. Did you (sea, see) the race between the (hare, hair) and the (foul, fowl)?
9. (Beet, Beat) the eggs before you add the (flower, flour).
10. The tent (steak, stake) was wet with (do, dew).
11. I will (meet, meat) you in the (meet, meat) department.
12. She forgot to (pour,poor) the milk before she (eight, ate).
13. (You're, Your) usually (pail, pale) when you are sick.
14. At the (fare, fair), I saw the dancing (bear, bare).
15. (Its, It's) impolite to (stair, stare).

FALL-OW THE BATS

Materials

navy blue or dark purple background
large, yellow, quarter-circle moon
orange letters spelling **Fall-ow the Bats**
bat pattern sheet (page 26)

Instructions

Put up the background. Add the moon and letters. By means of the photocopy or thermofax process, make copies of the bat pattern on page 26 and the project bats on page 27. Distribute the pattern sheets. Cut out the project bats and post them where children can see them easily or give each child his/her own copy.

Activities

- **Bats**—Help children assemble bats using the pattern pieces and instructions on page 26.
- **Batty Projects**—Allow sufficient class time for each child to complete one or more of the suggested projects independently. If all children are given a copy of the page, suggest that they keep track of their progress by coloring the corresponding bat each time they complete a project.

Name ______________________________

BAT PATTERN

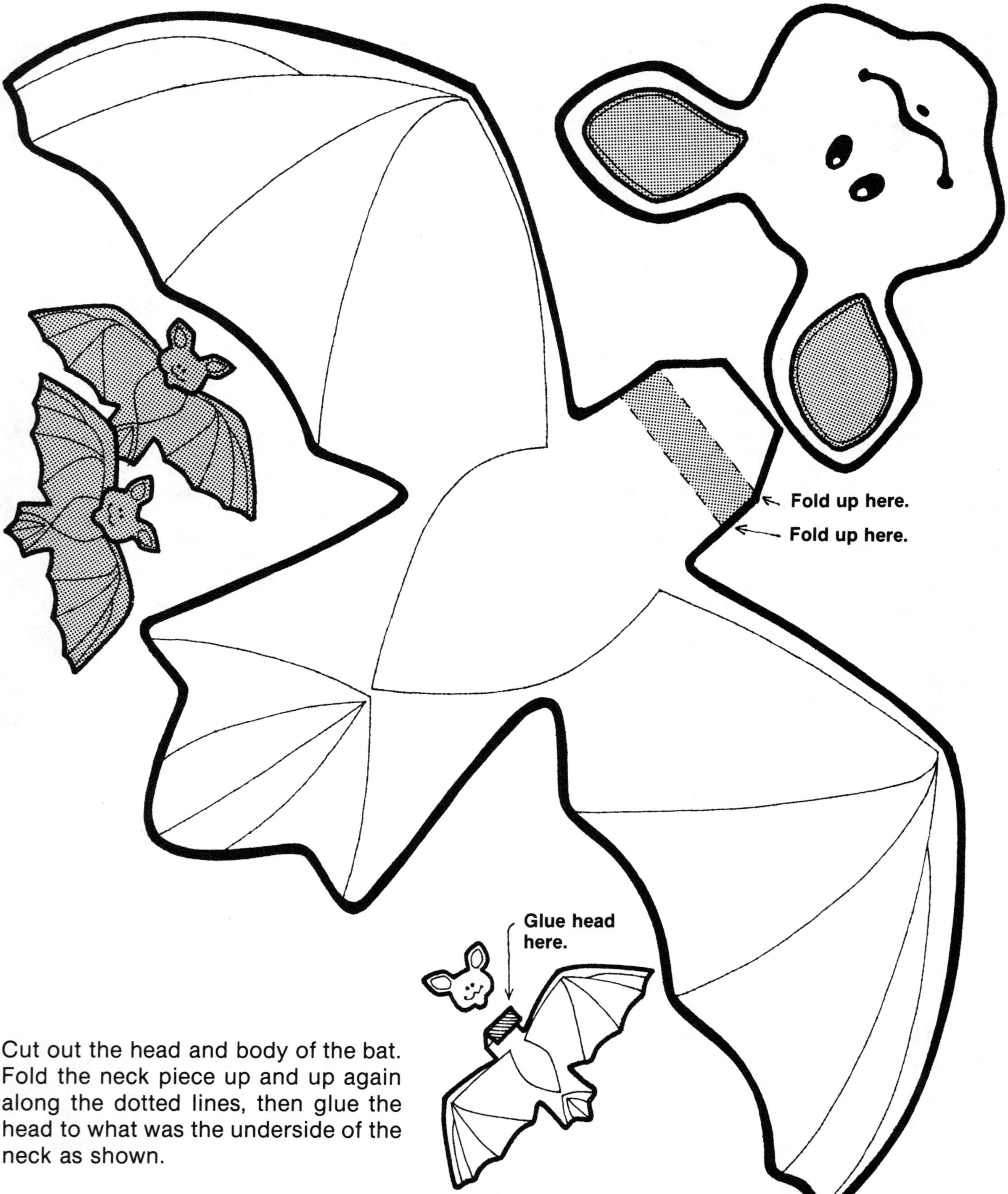

Cut out the head and body of the bat. Fold the neck piece up and up again along the dotted lines, then glue the head to what was the underside of the neck as shown.

Name ______________________________

BATTY PROJECTS

Design a bat mobile to hang near the bat bulletin board in your classroom.

On a sheet of paper, make a list of ten larger words that contain the smaller word **bat**. Then, write their dictionary definitions beside them. Examples: **bat**on, **bat**ik, **bat**tle

Design an imaginative bat cave. Label all of the rooms or sections appropriately with names such as the **batroom** and the **bat den**.

Boris the bat visited Dr. Dracula to find a cure for his phobia of dark places. Write a story explaining what a phobia is and what treatment the doctor prescribed.

Make a list of several things that drive you "batty."

BEST-DRESSED TURKEYS

Materials

yellow background
large, brown butcher paper sign on which are written the words
Ye Olde Fowl Fashion Dress Shoppe
brown letters spelling **Best-Dressed Turkeys**
pilgrim turkey pattern (pages 29 and 30)

Instructions

Put up the background. Add the sign and letters. Using the photocopy or thermofax process, make copies of the turkey pattern on pages 29 and 30 and of the food groups activity sheet on page 31.

Activities

- **Turkeys**—Have children carefully color, cut out, and assemble their "best-dressed" turkeys using the pattern pieces on pages 29 and 30.
- **Turkey Dressing**—If time permits, encourage children to design for their turkeys additional outfits, such as riding or hunting clothes, bathing suits, and pajamas.
- **Food Groups Activity Sheet**—Use the Gobbler's Inn Menu (page 31) to give children practice in matching listed items with the correct food groups.

Name ______________________________

PILGRIM TURKEY

Color and cut out the pieces on pages 29 and 30. Then, assemble and dress the turkey.

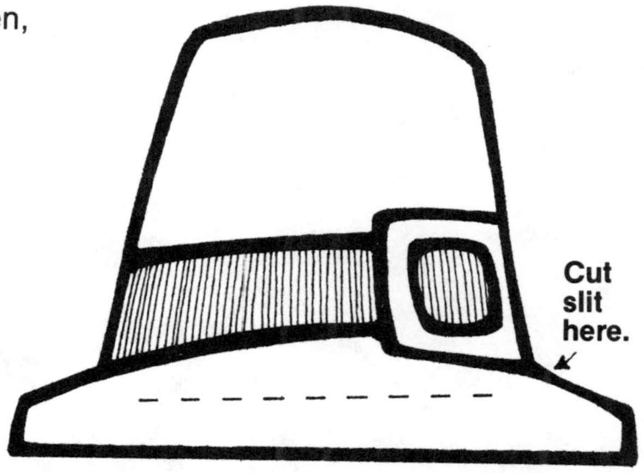

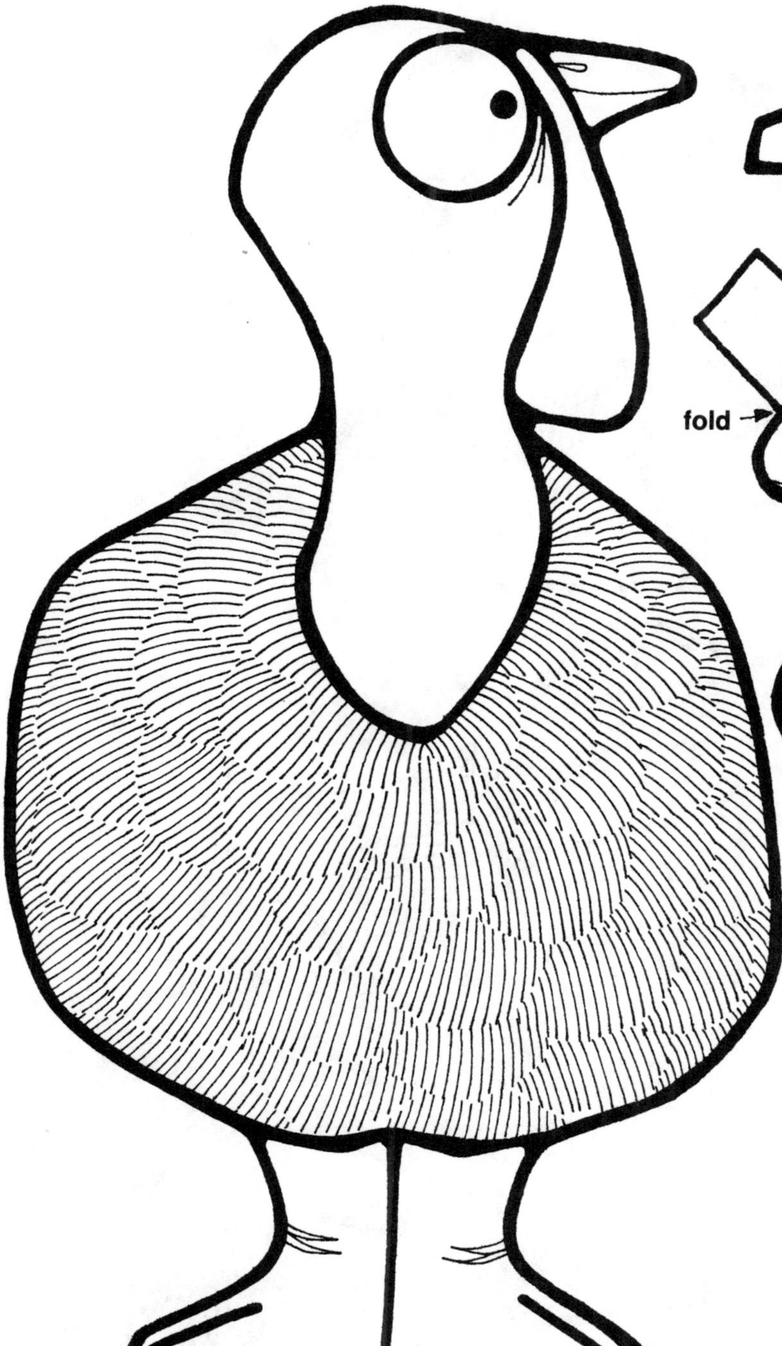

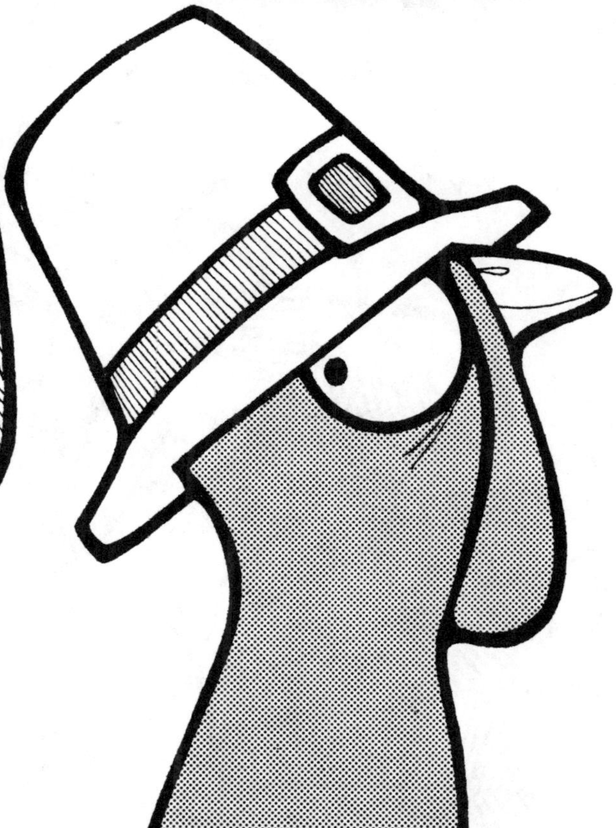

Name ______________________________

PILGRIM TURKEY (continued)

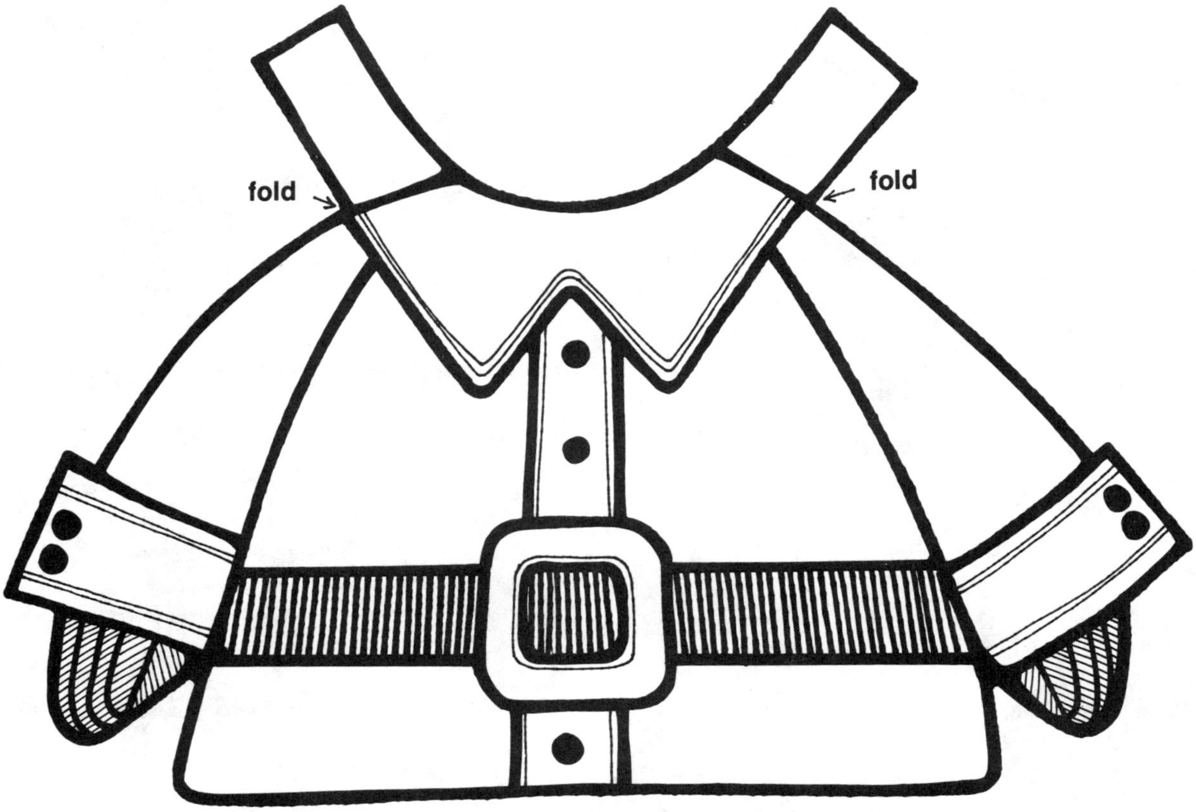

Glue tail feathers to back of turkey before dressing it.

Name ____________________

GOBBLER'S INN MENU

Today's Menu

Roast Turkey
Dressing
Cranberry Sauce
Mashed Potatoes
Turkey Gravy
Corn
Green Beans
Milk - Tea - Coffee
Hot Rolls
Butter
Pumpkin Pie

Write the name of each food listed on today's menu under the correct food group heading below.

Meat and Protein

____

____

Fruits and Vegetables

____

____

____

____

Milk and Dairy Products

____

____

Breads and Cereals

____

____

Other Foods

____

____

____

RAVEN HAVEN

Materials

yellow background
brown fence textured with darker brown or black ink or paint
black or brown letters spelling **Raven Haven**
black and orange construction paper for ravens
tagboard or construction paper for heads of scarecrows to be made by children
straw or pale yellow or gold construction paper for scarecrow arms and legs
two popsicle sticks or tongue depressors for each child

Instructions

Put up the background and add the fence, letters, and ravens. Using the photocopy or thermofax process, make copies of pages 33, 34, and 35 to use when doing the activities described below.

Activities

- **Scarecrows**—Help students assemble scarecrows following the instructions and using the pattern pieces on pages 33 and 34.
- **Raven's Rhymes Activity Sheet**—Complement your art lesson with an exercise in rhyme.

Name ____________________

SCARECROW'S HEAD

1. Carefully glue two popsicle sticks or tongue depressors together.

2. While the glue dries, color and cut out the scarecrow's clothes on page 34.

3. Fold the clothes along the dotted line.

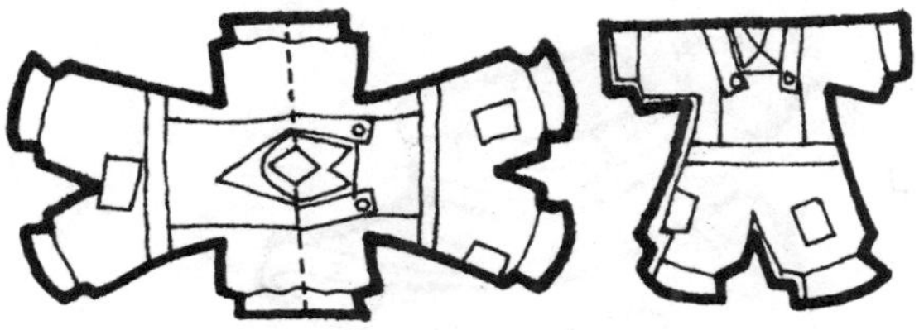

4. Cut out the neck opening.

5. Insert the vertical stick up through the neck opening and slide the clothes down until they rest on the horizontal stick.

6. Tuck straw or construction paper up sleeves and pant legs and glue in place on sticks.

7. Glue down the clothes.

8. Color and cut out the scarecrow's head at the top of this page.

9. Glue the head to the vertical stick.

Name ____________________

SCARECROW'S CLOTHES

Name ______________________

RAVEN'S RHYMES

On each of the second line blanks below, write a word that rhymes with the last word in the first line.

1. 'Tis the month of Halloween
   When ghosts are heard but can't be ________________.

2. Black cats prowling 'round at night,
   Making children run with ________________.

3. Autumn shines with gold and red.
   "A pretty season," the farmer ________________.

4. Hoot owls hoot; the wind does blow;
   A-trick-or-treating we will ________________.

5. Scarecrows with your arms of straw—
   What a picture for me to ________________.

6. Our garden fence stands straight and tall.
   It keeps out rabbits large and ________________.

7. Pumpkins for gals, pumpkins for guys,
   Pumpkins to carve or to make into ________________.

8. I want the mask of a witch or a queen,
   So on Halloween night, my face won't be ________________.

9. I saw a witch on her broom in the sky.
   She scared me so much that I thought I would ________________.

10. A pumpkin sitting on the barnyard gate
    Will be lit at half past ________________.

11. Dressed in my costume, carrying my sack...
    Don't worry, Mom, I'll soon be ________________.

12. A sack full of candy, an apple or two...
    I like you so much that I'll share it with ________________.

A SALUTE TO NOVEMBER

Materials

chicken wire backing
red, white, or blue construction paper letters that spell **A Salute to November** to be placed on the wall above the display
one large white cardboard star to be placed on the blue field of the flag
red, white, and blue crepe or tissue paper for making flowers
twist ties or florist's wire for use in tying paper flowers and attaching them to the wire backing

Instructions

Staple the chicken wire to the board. Attach the letters to the board or to the wall above the wire backing. Make available crepe or tissue paper rectangles cut to approximately 8 by 24 or 10 by 30 inches and twist ties or florist's wire.

Activities

- **Paper Flowers**—Have children follow the instructions on page 37 to make paper flowers for the flag.
- **Flag Facts**—Allow time for children to proofread this activity sheet and correct the misspelled words.

Note: This bulletin board display could be used as **A Salute to June** and **Flag Day** (June 14).

Name ______________________

PAPER FLOWERS

1. Cut crepe or tissue paper into 8-by-24- or 10-by-30-inch rectangles.

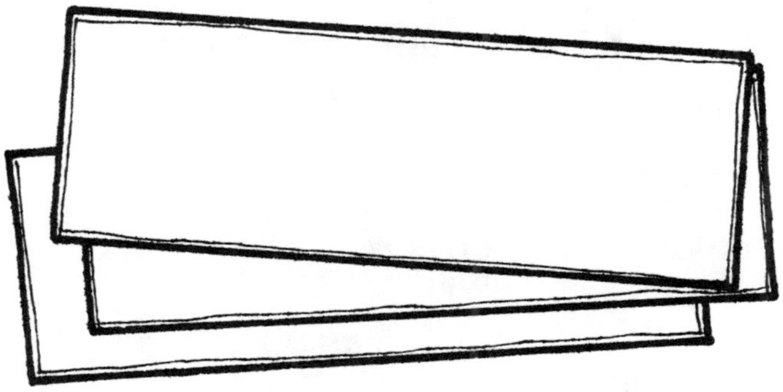

2. Fold each rectangle in half so that it measures 8 by 12 or 10 by 15 inches.

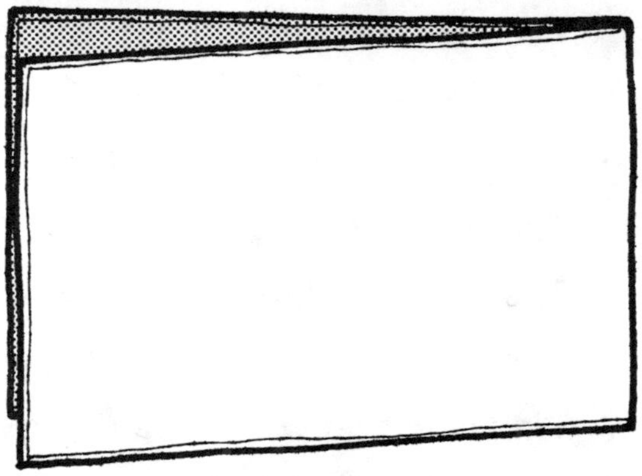

3. Carefully hand gather the folded paper at its center.

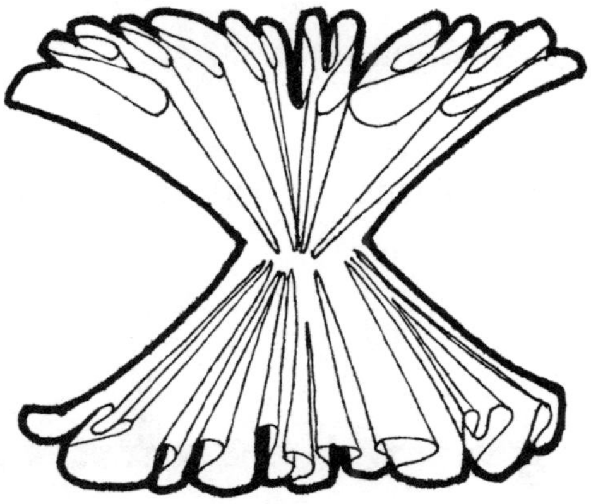

4. Tie the gathered flower with florist's wire or a twist tie.

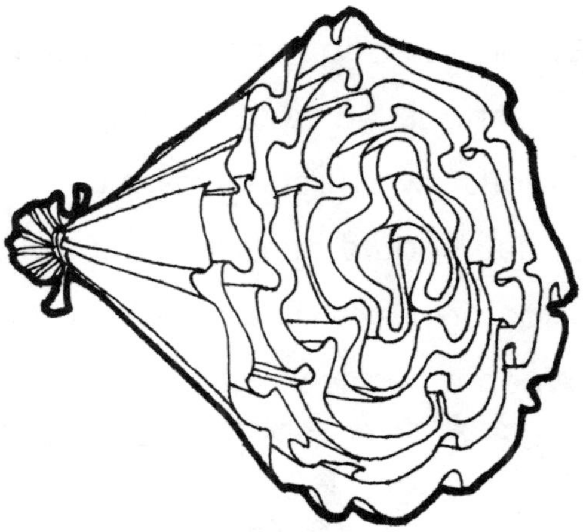

5. Insert your completed flower in the wire frame and secure it if necessary with florist's wire or a twist tie.

Name ____________________

FLAG FACTS

Locate and correct all of the misspelled words in the sentences below.

1. Our flag is sometimes calld the "Stars an Stripes."
2. Our flag stans for the American people, their land, and there government.
3. Their have ben many flags representing are country.
4. The Amercan flag that we use today is red, wite, and blue.
5. The strips on the flag represnt the thirteen original colonys.
6. The stars represent are fiftie states.
7. We show that we are patriotik when we saloot the flag.
8. Usally, we display the flag only in fair whether.
9. Your hand shood be placed over your hart when you salute the flag.
10. When sumone famous dies, our flag is offen flown at half-mast.
11. At school, we say the "Plege of Alegiance."
12. Our flag was first flown on the moon in 1969 buy Neel Armstrong and Edwin Aldrin.
13. A flag should be razed quickly and lowerd slowly.
14. A color-bearer is a person who caries the flag.
15. When a flag is worn-out, it shoud be burned.

SHINING BRIGHTLY

Materials

dark blue background
pale blue crepe paper for curtains
rectangular strip of white construction paper for the windowsill
dark blue letters to spell **Shining Brightly**
silver, gold, or brown paper for the large menorah
empty paper towel rolls or other cardboard tubes for the candles
aluminum foil or foil wrapping paper to wrap the candles
additional materials, such as yarn, ribbon, or rickrack for decorating the candles if desired
yellow construction paper for candle flames

Instructions

Put up the background. Pleat crepe paper and staple it to the board to form curtains as shown. Add the windowsill, letters, and menorah. By means of the photocopy or thermofax process, make copies of the candle instructions and flame pattern on page 40 and the activity sheets on pages 41 and 42 to use when you do the activities described below.

Activities

- **Candles**—Have students bring empty paper towel rolls or other cardboard tubes from home and then follow the pattern and instructions on the Create a Candle sheet (page 40) to make and decorate their own foil-covered Hanukkah candles.
- **Punctuation Activity Sheet**—Complement this holiday craft lesson with the Shining Sentences activity sheet on page 41.
- **Declare a Holiday**—Suggest that students use the activity sheet on page 42 to create, describe, and declare their own special holidays.

Name ______________________

CREATE A CANDLE

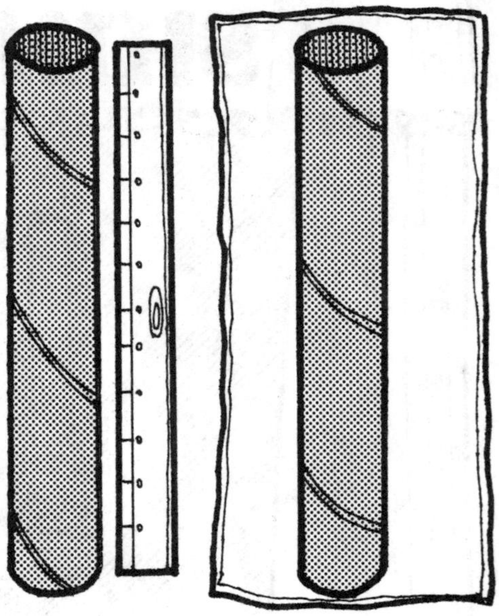

1. Bring an empty paper towel roll or other cardboard tube from home.
2. Measure the length of the tube and write that measurement here.

   Length = ______________ inches
3. Measure the circumference of the tube and write that measurement here.

   Circumference = _________ inches
4. Add one inch to each measurement.

   Length = 1 inch + _______ inches
   Circumference = 1 inch + _______ inches

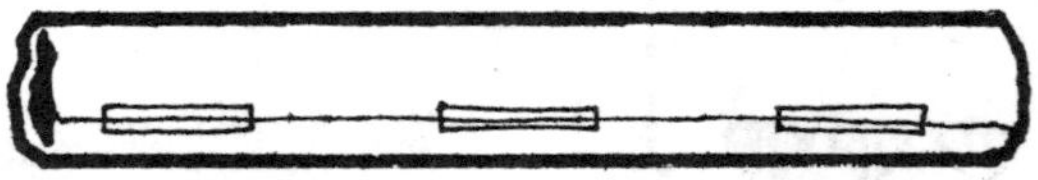

5. Cut a piece of aluminum foil or foil wrapping paper that is as long as your new length and as wide as your new circumference.
6. Lay the cardboard tube on the paper so that there is an extra one-half inch at the top and the bottom.
7. Wrap the paper tightly around the tube.
8. Secure the paper by tucking the overlap inside the tube at the top and bottom and by taping or gluing the seam.
9. Color the flame on this page and cut it out.
10. Stick the tab down inside the foil-wrapped tube.
11. Tape or glue the tab in place if necessary.
12. Decorate your foil candle with pieces of yarn, ribbon, felt scraps, or rickrack if you wish.

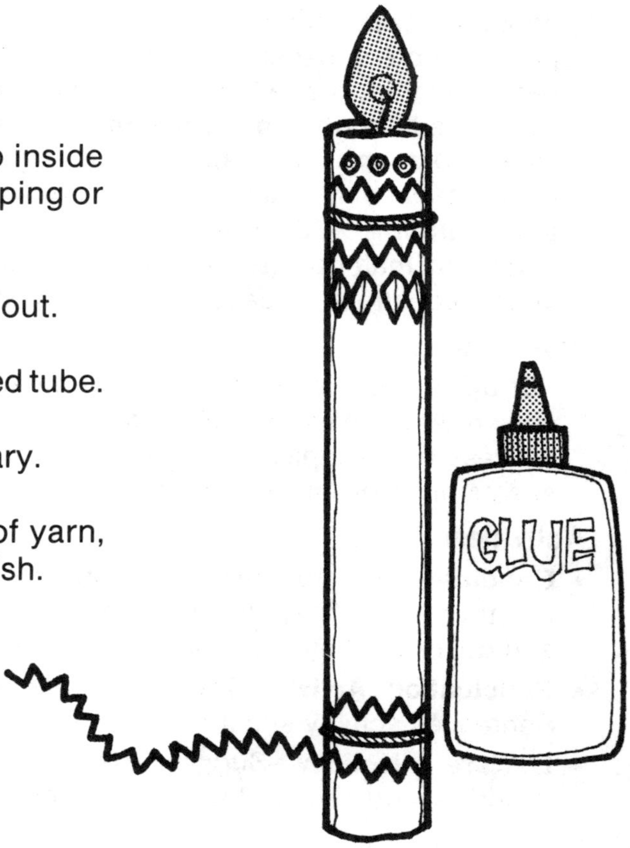

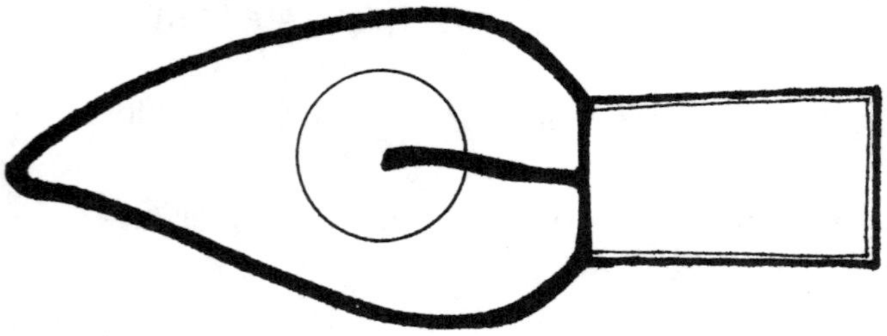

Name ______________________________

SHINING SENTENCES

Punctuate each of these sentences. As your teacher reads the correct punctuation, check to see how many of them you got right. Color the candle of each sentence you punctuated correctly.

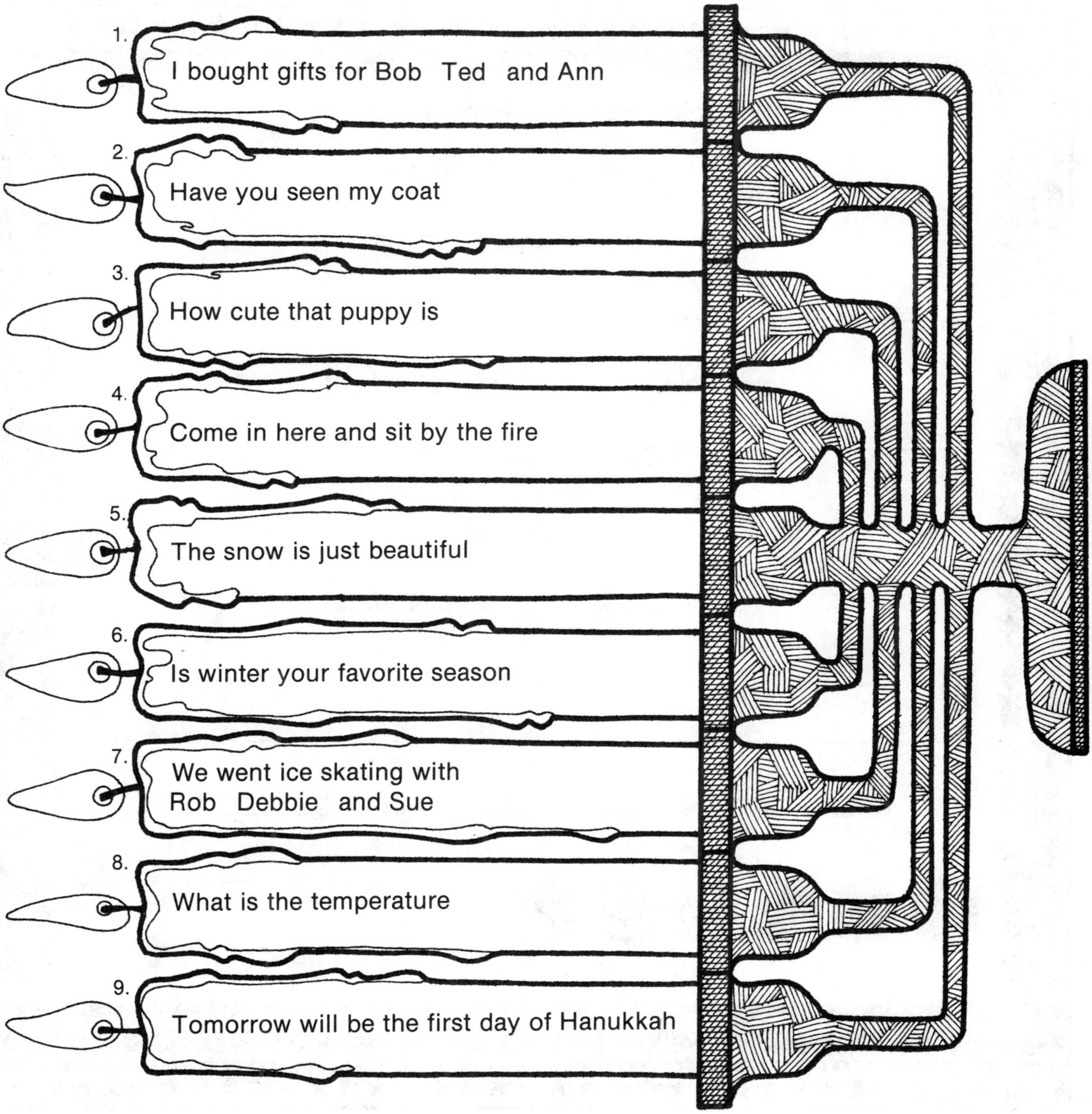

Name ____________________

DECLARE A HOLIDAY

Throughout the world, people celebrate holidays because a governor, president, king, or church official has decided that one was needed and has proclaimed it. Pretend that you are in a position to declare a holiday. Fill in the proclamation below by naming your holiday and telling when, by whom, how it is to be celebrated, and whom it will honor.

Official Holiday Proclamation

I do hereby proclaim that

____
(month, date)

shall henceforth and forever be called

____
(name of holiday)

to be celebrated throughout the land by

____
(Name the group your holiday is to be celebrated by, for example, children, women, men, or everyone.)

in honor of

____
(Name the group your holiday is intended to honor, for example, mothers, children, teachers, or pets.)

with ______________________________

____

____
(Describe the ways in which your holiday should be celebrated, for example, with dancing and feasting, with singing, or with total silence.)

____
(signature)

____
(date)

SILENT NIGHT

Materials

dark blue background
white letters spelling **Silent Night**
white paint or chalk for drawing the musical staff and treble clef
angel hair or fluffy cotton for clouds
foil-covered cardboard stars
tagboard for angels to be made by students using the patterns on page 44
cotton balls or pale yellow yarn for angels' hair
white paper doilies for angels' dresses (Two large doilies are needed for each angel.)
gold or silver star stickers in assorted sizes to decorate angels' dresses
glitter to decorate angels' wings and halos, if desired

Instructions

Put up the background. Add the staff, treble clef, and letters. Attach clouds and foil-covered stars. By means of the photocopy or thermofax process, make copies of the angel pattern and instructions on pages 44 and 45 and of the activity sheet on page 46. Hand one to each member of your class as you prepare to do the activities described below.

Activities

- **Angels**—Help children assemble angels using the pattern pieces and instructions on pages 44 and 45.
- **Attention: Angels**—Fill free time before the holidays with the holiday word search on page 46.

Name ______________________________

ANGEL PATTERN

Name ____________________

ANGEL INSTRUCTIONS

1. Cut out the body, halo, and wing pieces on page 44.

2. Place each of these pattern pieces on tagboard and draw around it.

3. Cut out the resulting tagboard shapes.

4. Using felt-tipped pens, crayons, or colored pencils, draw a face on the head portion of the body.

5. To create gown back, fold one doily in half.

6. Cut a circular neckhole that is at least 1-5/8 inches wide.

Step 6

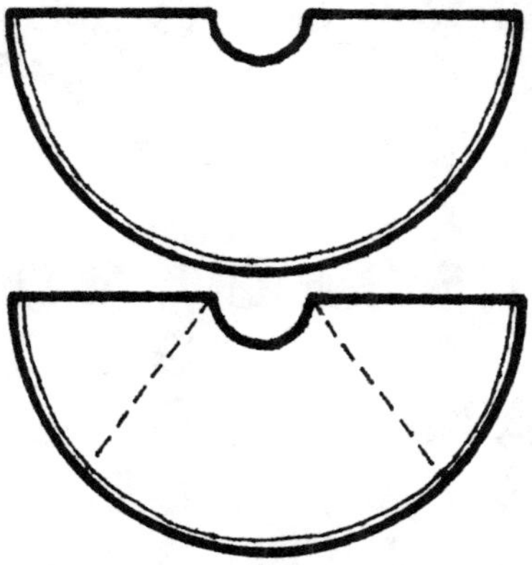

7. Fold over the edges of the doily to create sleeves.

Step 7

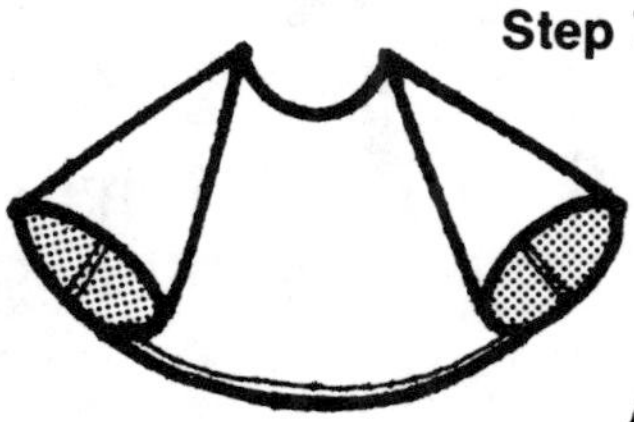

8. Make the skirt and gown front by folding the second doily to create an A-line as shown, leaving at least a 1-5/8 inch neckhole.

Step 8

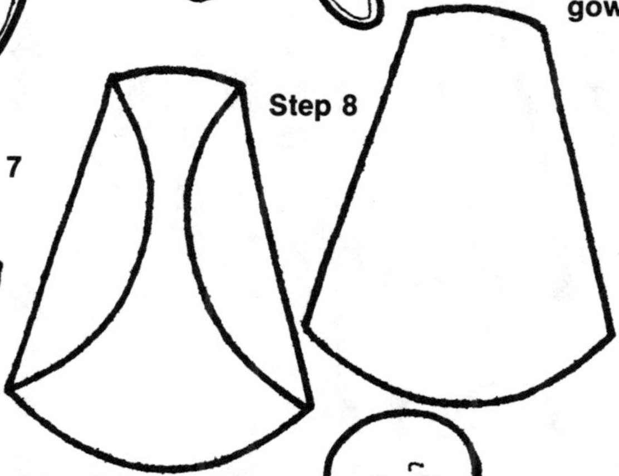

inside of gown front

outside of gown front

9. Carefully glue gown front to front of angel.

Step 9

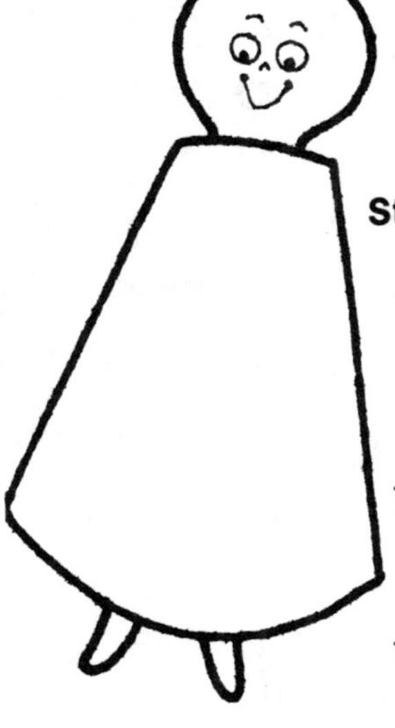

10. Carefully glue gown back to back of angel, allowing sleeves to overlap gown front.

Step 10

11. Glue cotton balls or yarn around edge of face for hair.

12. Glue halo to back of head.

13. Glue or staple wings to back of angel.

Name ______________________________

ATTENTION: ANGELS

Circle all of the holiday words that you find in the angel puzzle below. They read horizontally, vertically, and diagonally, and from right to left and bottom to top. All twenty-two words are listed at the bottom of the page.

```
T X C Y
R O N L S M
J S P L T U T B
S T O C K I N G
G M H I M O T H E C
D I N R A D C A
Y S P B G R
B U R   U E T S O U   N C B
W R E A T H T X L J R X Y E J L
D U B V I D T S S E C A N D R A
R D Y G E A I A N N T G L O L V
R O W X D E A M I N B O U L F R
J L N I K E S T A R G L E O W E
N P L A C R Q S L O U B I S T B
L H L C S T N I C H O L A S G M
E X M E L I S R S A K I M B Q E
H B K K U N B H J X Y T A S T C
G I T S B V T C A N D Y C A N E
A J E T A T S Y X K S A J I E D
L F R O G N E R L X K P T R M F
M E N Y M E G R Y G R B N A A Z
C A Q C H E S R E L D N A C I N C S
P H M I A D E T M L B R I F N R I D
N A T O M E R F R A N C B S H O U P
W B N D A P L I O U E X J S K P
```

ornament	piñata			joy	peace
St. Nicholas	angel	candle	mistletoe	Rudolph	holly
Merry Christmas	tree	stocking	poinsettia	bell	present
Santa	star	December	candy cane	wreath	carols

NOT A CREATURE WAS STIRRING . . .

Materials

red or pale green background
white letters spelling **Not a Creature Was Stirring . . . Not Even a Mouse**
dark green construction paper for holly leaves
red construction paper for holly berries
at least one uncooked egg for each child
darning needle or other similar sharp object for making holes in eggs
cups or bowls to hold blown egg whites and yolks
gray dye or tempera paint
gray and pink construction paper or felt for mouse ears
pieces of thick yarn approximately 4 inches long for mouse tails
black construction paper for eyes and noses (The plastic eyes with movable pupils found in many craft stores may also be used.)
black pipe cleaners or construction paper for whiskers

Instructions

Put up the background. Add letters and holly. Using the photocopy or thermofax process, make copies of the mouse pattern on page 48. Fill in the activity sheet on page 49 and copy it also. Attach student-made mice to the board by their tails. Display completed activity sheets there also.

Activities

- **Mice**—Help children assemble mice using the pattern pieces and instructions on page 48.
- **Multipurpose Mice**—Use this mouse activity sheet to complement your mouse art project. Simply write a title on the line at the top and then write a math problem, spelling word, or activity idea on each mouse.

Name ____________________

MOUSE PATTERN

1. Make a small hole in one end of your egg with a darning needle.
2. Make a slightly larger hole in the opposite end of your egg.
3. Hold your egg over a cup or bowl and blow through the smaller hole until all of the white and yolk come out the larger hole.
4. Allow the empty eggshell to dry.
5. Immerse the empty shell in gray dye or tempera paint.

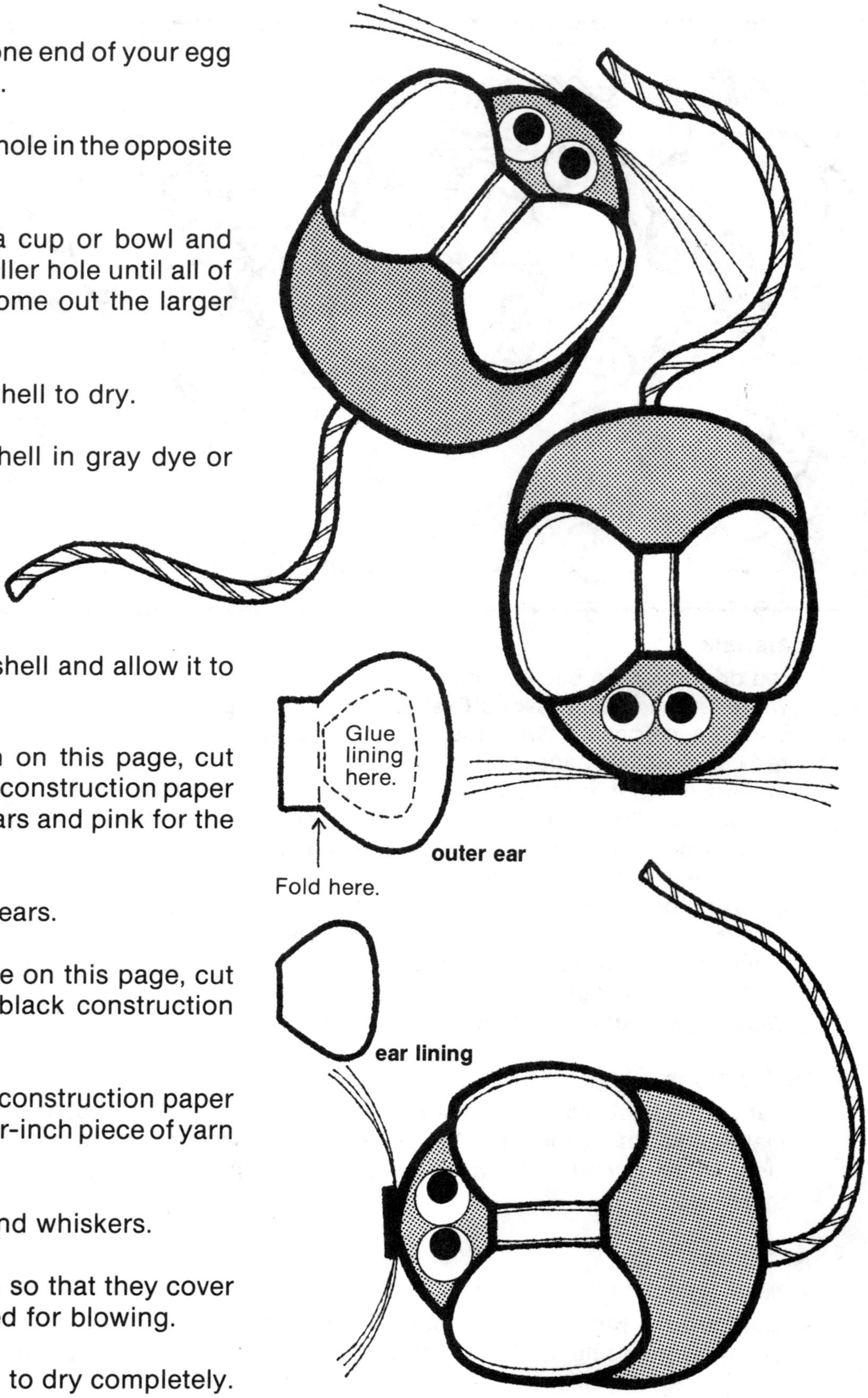

6. Remove the colored shell and allow it to dry completely.
7. Following the pattern on this page, cut mouse ears. Use gray construction paper or felt for the outer ears and pink for the linings.
8. Glue linings to outer ears.
9. Following the example on this page, cut eyes and nose from black construction paper.
10. Use pipe cleaners or construction paper for whiskers and a four-inch piece of yarn for the tail.
11. Glue on ears, eyes, and whiskers.
12. Glue on nose and tail so that they cover the openings you used for blowing.
13. Allow finished mouse to dry completely.

Name ______________________________

____

CHIME TIME

Materials

yellow background
brown letters spelling **Chime Time**
large grandfather clock cut from butcher or construction paper with brown frame; white face; black numbers, eyes, and dots; gold pendulum; and white or brown arms
actual party hat, horn, and streamers for a three-dimensional effect
brown, yellow, black, and gray construction paper for smaller clocks and mice to be made by students

Instructions

Put up the background. Add the letters, the large grandfather clock, and the hat, horn, and streamers. By means of the photocopy or thermofax process, make copies of clock and mice patterns on pages 51-53 and of the activity sheets on pages 54 and 55 to use when you do the activities described below.

Activities

- **Clocks with Mice**—Help children assemble clocks with mice using the instructions and pattern pieces on pages 51-53. Allow each child time to write a resolution on his mouse.
- **On Time**—After explaining or reviewing how to tell time using a conventional clock, reinforce the lesson with this activity sheet on which children draw clock faces to match specified times.
- **Wintertime**—Use this activity sheet to familiarize children with pronunciation guides and reinforce dictionary skills.

Name ______________________

MOUSE SHAPE AND CLOCK INSTRUCTIONS

1. Cut clock box from brown construction paper using the pattern on page 52.
2. Following the patterns on page 53, cut out black hands and weights and a yellow face for your clock.
3. Using a black crayon or felt-tipped marking pen, add numbers to the face of your clock.
4. Glue the weights to the bottom edge of the clock box back.

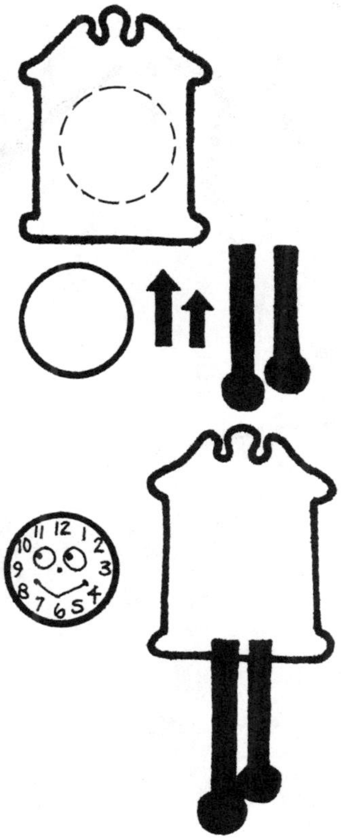

5. Turn the clock box over and glue the face to the center of the box within the dotted circle.
6. Glue the hands to the center of the face.
7. Write a New Year's resolution on the mouse below.
8. Glue your resolution mouse to the clock's right weight.

Write one New Year's resolution inside this mouse. Then, cut it out and glue it to your clock in the position shown.

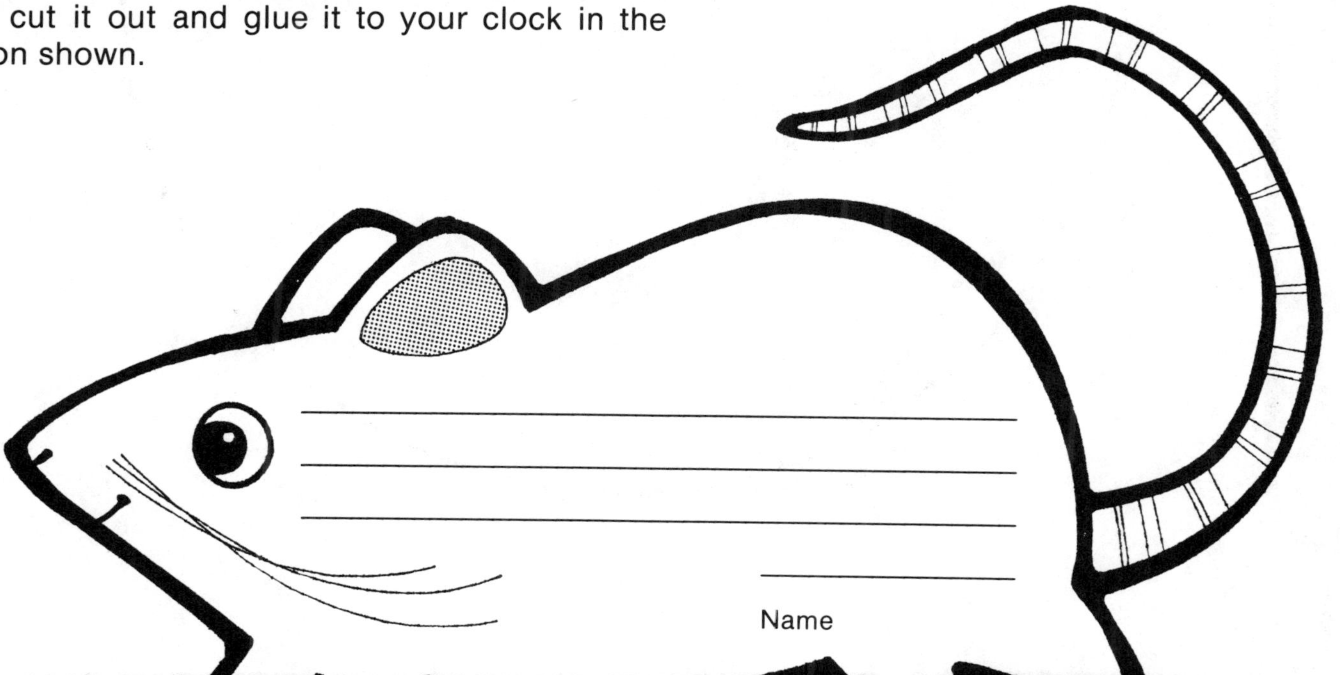

Name ______________________

CLOCK PATTERN

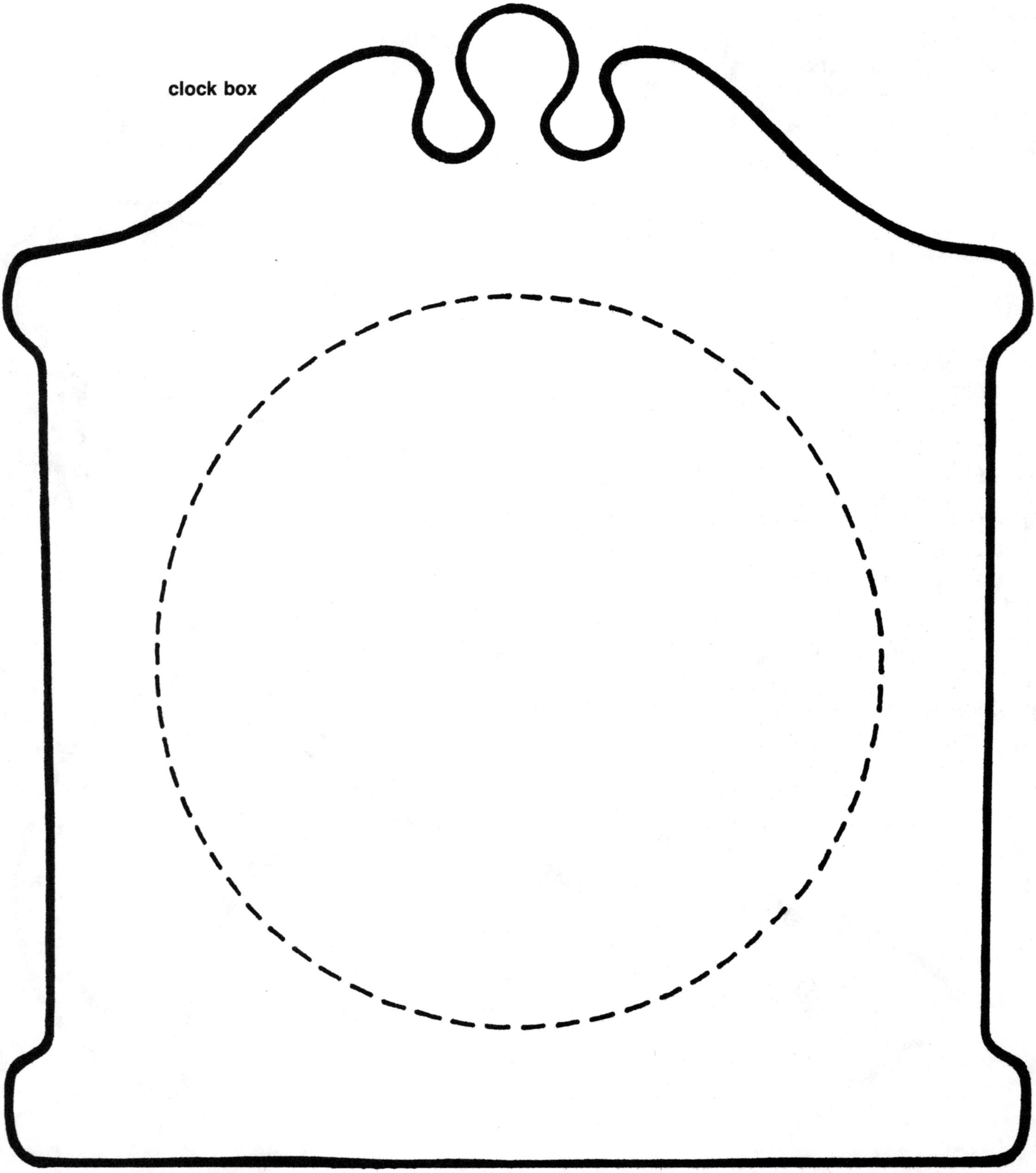

Cut from brown construction paper.

Name ______________________

CLOCK PATTERN

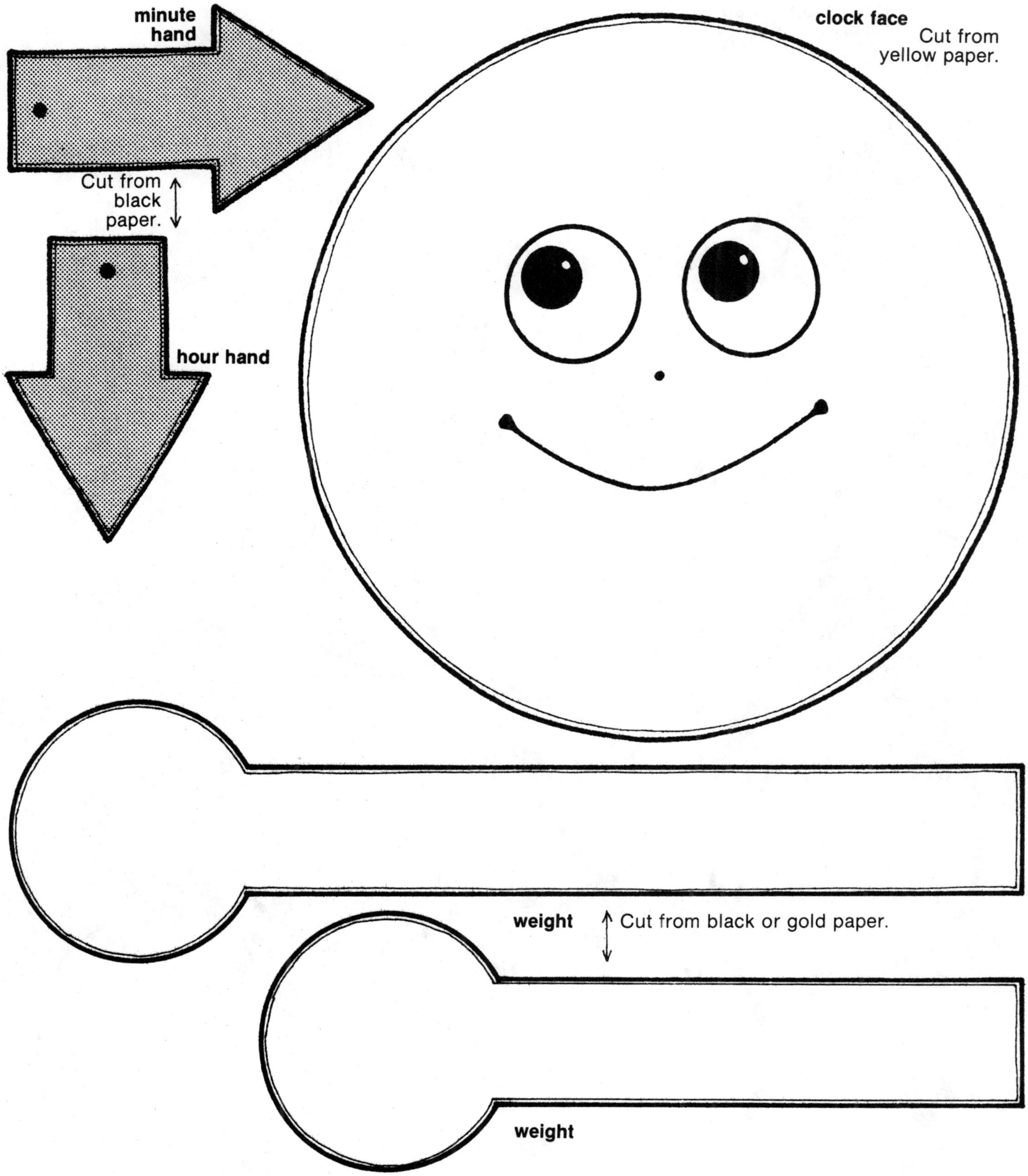

Name ______________________

ON TIME

Draw hands on these clock faces to represent the times written below them.

Name ______________________________

WINTERTIME

Use the pronunciation guides in your dictionary to locate the correct spellings of the words in the sentences below.

1. Jăn′ yo͝o ĕr ĭ ĭz thə fûrst mŭnth.

____

2. Ī mād ə rĕz ə lo͝o′ shə n.

____

3. No͝o Yĭr′z Dā ĭz Jăn. 1.

____

4. Ĭt ĭz prĭt′ ĭ hwĕn ĭt snōz.

____

5. Wĭn′ tər ĭz mī fā′v ə r ĭt sē zən.

____

6. Thə rōdz gĕt vĕr ē ī sē.

____

7. Ŏn băd dāz, thêr ĭz nō sko͞ol.

____

8. No͝o Yĭr′z Dā ĭz ə wĭn′ tər hŏl′ ə dā.

____

9. Sŭm tīmz wē skāt ŏn thə pŏnd.

____

10. Mī frĕndz ănd Ī līk to͝o rīd ŏn slĕdz.

____

A COLD CATCH

Materials

dark blue background for sky
light blue background for water
white snowbank with black pen marks to further suggest snowdrifts
large white polar bear outlined in black to accentuate his shape and features and distinguish him from the white snowbank on which he sits
a lightweight fishing pole or a wooden dowel wrapped with fishing line or string
white letters spelling **A Cold Catch**
white ditto or photocopy paper for fish to be made by students

Instructions

Put up the dark blue background and then the light blue background. Add snowbank, bear, pole, and line. Staple letters to sky portion of display. By means of the photocopy or thermofax process, make copies of the activity sheets on pages 57, 58, and 59. Hand one copy of each sheet to each member of your class as you prepare to do the activities described below.

Activities

- **Polar Fish**—Help children make origami fish using the pattern and instructions on page 57.
- **Math Activity Sheet**—As a test or reinforcement of basic addition skills, have children complete the Catch a Sum activity sheet on page 58. For an added challenge, have them work against a timer or the clock.
- **Health Activity Sheet**—Because January is a month during which many people catch colds, increase student awareness of health preservation and disease prevention with the Catch-a-Cold activity sheet on page 59.

Name ______________________________

ORIGAMI POLAR FISH PATTERN

Origami is the Japanese art of paper folding. Using crayons, felt-tipped marking pens, or colored pencils, create and color an original design in the square below. Then, follow the instructions to fold this square into an origami polar fish.

1. Fold square to triangle shape. Crease along broken lines.

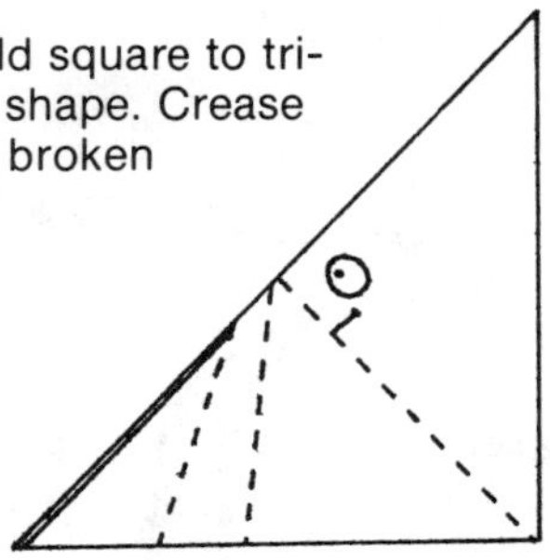

2. Cut slit and fold up *one* tail piece.

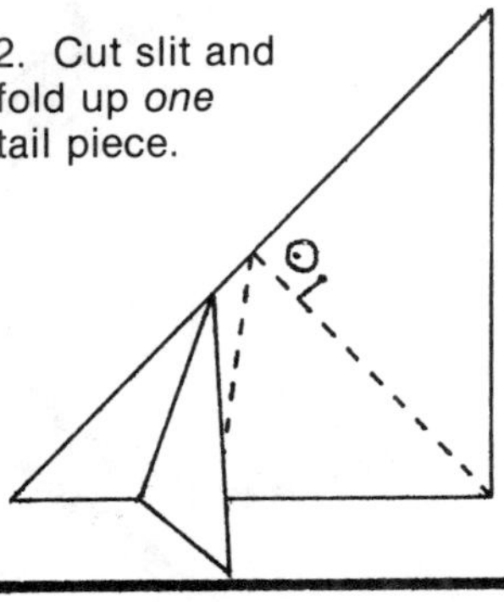

3. Fold both tail pieces up into fish body.

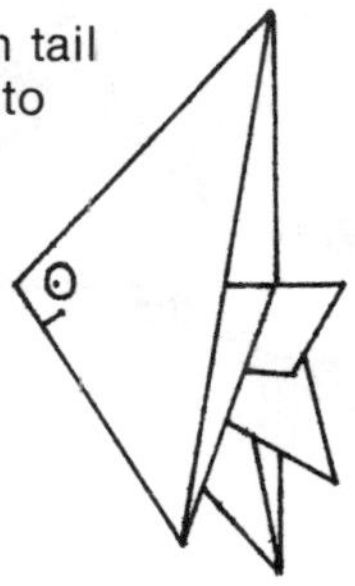

4. Fold up fins on front and back. Add earmuffs if you like.

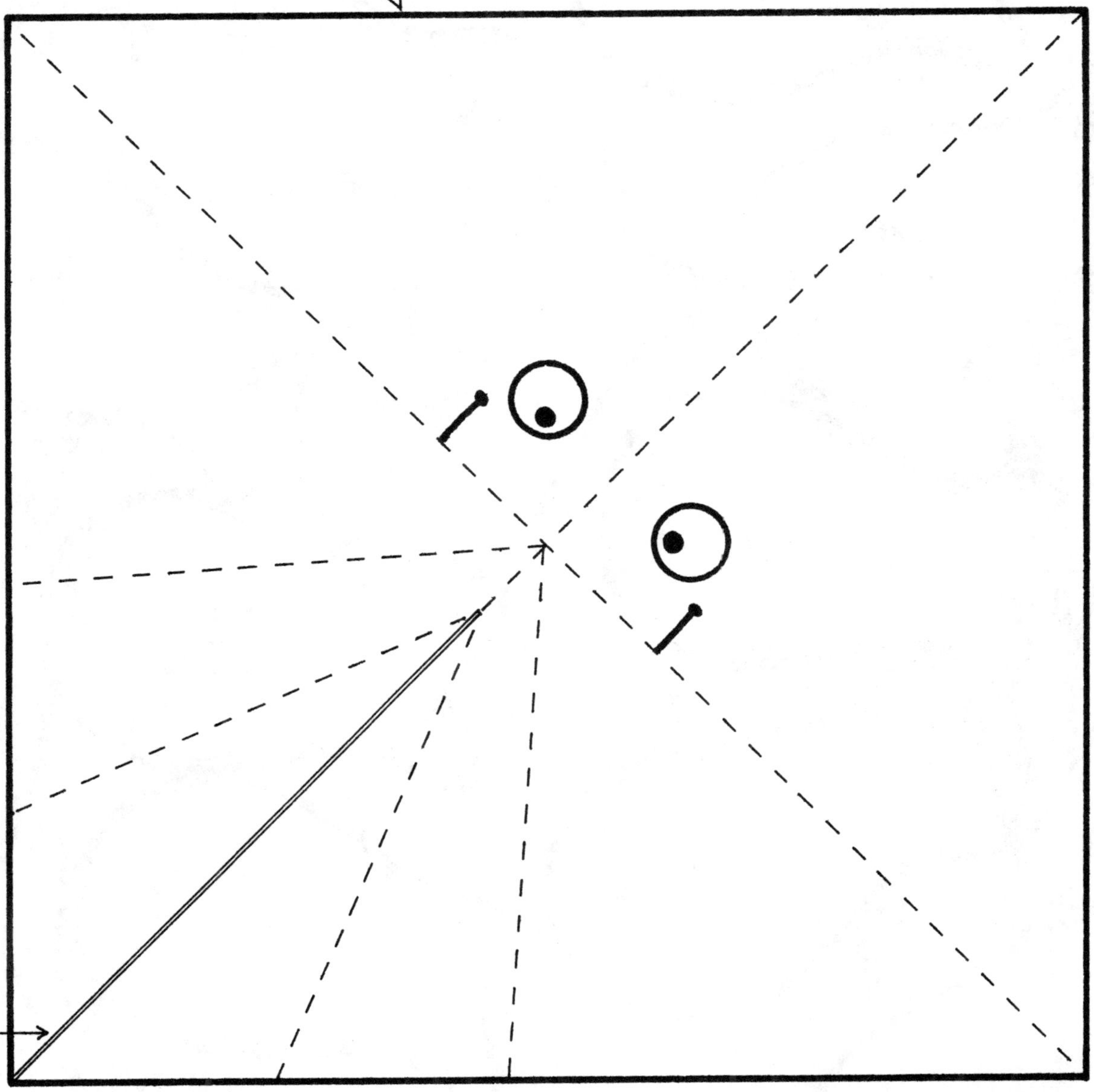

Cut slit here.

Name ______________________

CATCH A SUM

Name ____________________

IT'S CATCH-A-COLD TIME!

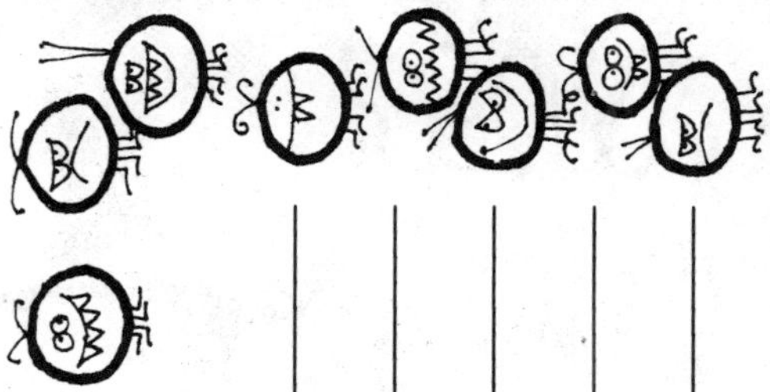

Pretend that you are a germ. Write a story about your life and what you like to do.

This self-portrait shows how I look when I have a cold.

When I catch a cold, ____________________

WE ARE FAMILY

Materials

dark blue background for sky
white letters spelling **We Are Family**
white puffs of drifted snow made either from white paper or fluffy sheet cotton
assorted colors of construction paper for students to use in making torn-paper snow people and clothing for them

Instructions

Put up sky. Add white letters and drifted snow. Using the photocopy or thermofax process, make copies of pages 61 and 62 to use when doing the activities described below.

Activities

- **Snow People**—Keep the scissors out of reach for this activity. No cutting allowed! Help students create and dress their own torn-paper snow people following the instructions on page 61.
- **Word Families**—Complement your art lesson with the word search language arts activity sheet on page 62.

Name ______________________

TORN-PAPER SNOW PEOPLE

1. Put your scissors away. No cutting allowed!

2. From a sheet of white construction paper, tear a single large snow person or a family of smaller snow people.

3. In the same way, tear construction paper of other colors to create hats, shirts, dresses, scarves, and facial features.

4. Glue these decorations to your snow figure or members of your snow family.

Name ______________________________

WORD FAMILIES

In the word search puzzle below, locate and draw a ring around each of the words that is printed in one of the surrounding word family circles. Remember to look horizontally, vertically, and diagonally, and to read from right to left and from bottom to top.

Colors

purple
black
white
orange
yellow
brown

Vegetables

beans
corn
beets
lettuce
pepper
carrot

L	T	I	B	B	A	R	S	N	I	T
A	K	C	A	L	B	D	V	G	C	Y
W	S	E	L	T	R	U	T	S	A	M
O	G	C	E	H	O	S	L	F	R	A
L	W	H	T	X	Y	T	R	P	R	W
L	H	G	T	C	H	E	E	R	O	S
E	I	L	U	B	E	E	L	N	T	R
Y	T	E	C	Z	R	B	S	L	U	E
S	E	G	E	L	P	R	U	P	O	P
C	K	N	Y	E	L	O	R	W	X	P
T	R	A	G	O	D	W	D	T	Z	E
S	X	R	T	G	E	N	A	R	L	P
N	R	O	C	E	L	C	I	C	I	O
T	X	O	F	N	S	S	N	A	E	B

Winter

sled
ice
snow
skate
freeze
icicle

Animals

rabbit
bird
dog
turtle
cat
fox

BY GEORGE

Materials

pale green background
brown butcher paper tree trunk and branches textured with darker brown or black ink or paint
brown letters spelling **By George**
small brown-and-gray or brown-and-silver foil paper hatchet (A plastic tomahawk or toy hatchet may be used to create a three-dimensional effect.)
tagboard or white construction paper for cherries, leaves, and stems
red, green, and brown construction paper for children to use in covering cherries, leaves, and stems

Instructions

Put up the background. Add tree trunk and branches, hatchet, and letters. Using the photocopy or thermofax process, make copies of pages 64 and 65 to use when you do the activities described below.

Activities

- **Cherries, Stems, and Leaves**—Help children use the pattern on page 64 to create their own clusters of cherries.
- **Math Activity Sheet**—As a complement to your February art lesson, have children complete the Bowl of Cherries subtraction activity sheet on page 65. If these problems are inappropriate for your class, substitute other math problems, spelling or vocabulary words, or activity ideas before copying the sheet.

CHERRY PATTERN

Using this pattern, cut bunches of cherries from white tagboard or stiff construction paper. Then, have children tear bits of green, brown, and red construction paper and glue them to the leaves, stems, and fruit. Filling in cherry clusters may be an individual or small-group project. Encourage children to add their finished artwork to the **By George** board.

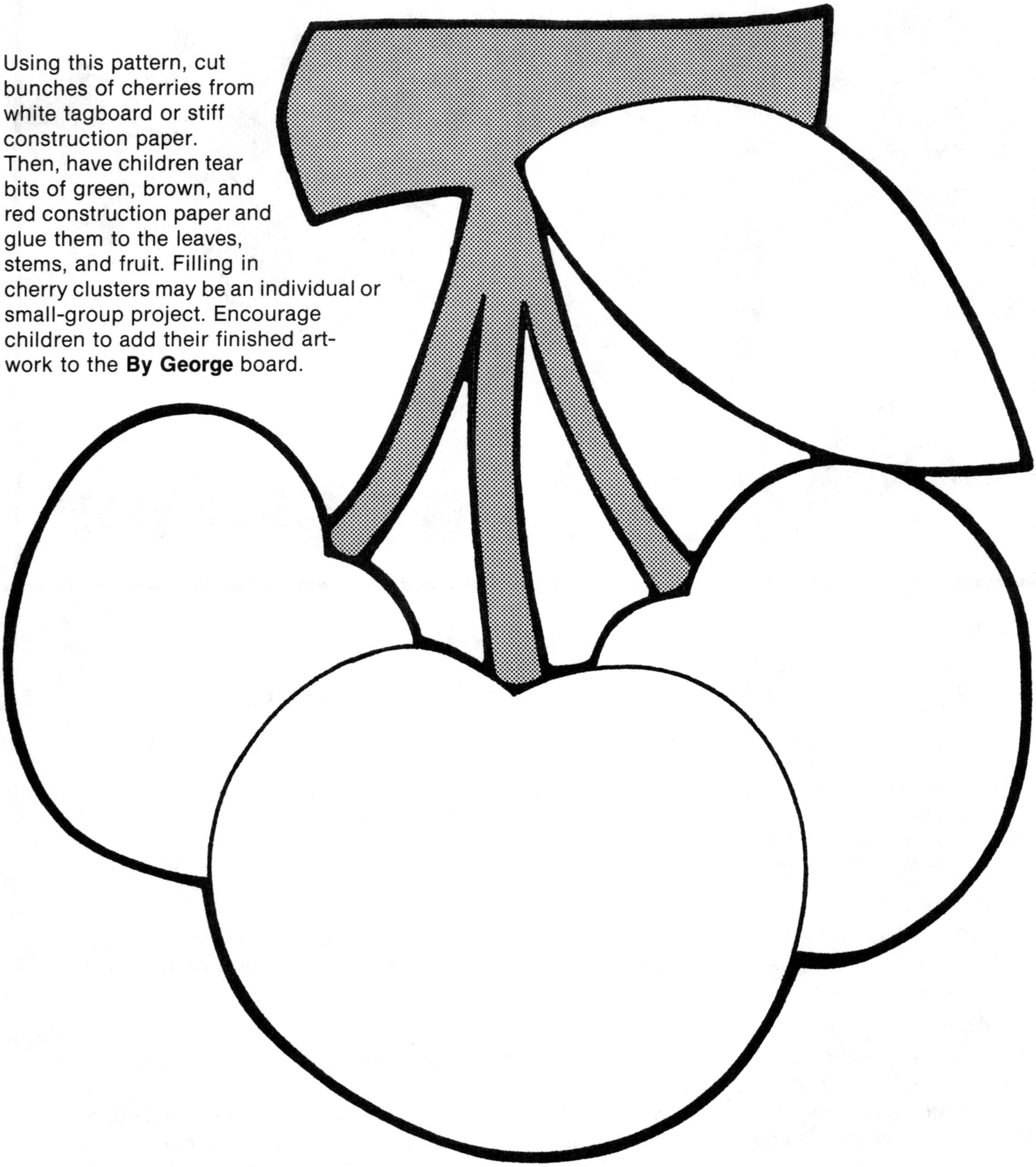

Name ____________________

A BOWL OF CHERRIES

Solve each of the subtraction problems below. Then, check your answers either by listening as your teacher reads the correct ones aloud or by comparing your answers with those in the answer key provided. Color each of the cherries in which the answer is correct. Cut the colored cherries out and glue them onto the bowl.

1. $751 - 238$
2. $462 - 279$
3. $376 - 194$
4. $825 - 537$
5. $294 - 137$
6. $962 - 139$
7. $578 - 329$
8. $452 - 273$
9. $391 - 187$
10. $566 - 347$
11. $883 - 494$
12. $429 - 157$
13. $250 - 172$
14. $573 - 384$
15. $625 - 483$
16. $573 - 284$
17. $789 - 259$
18. $306 - 199$

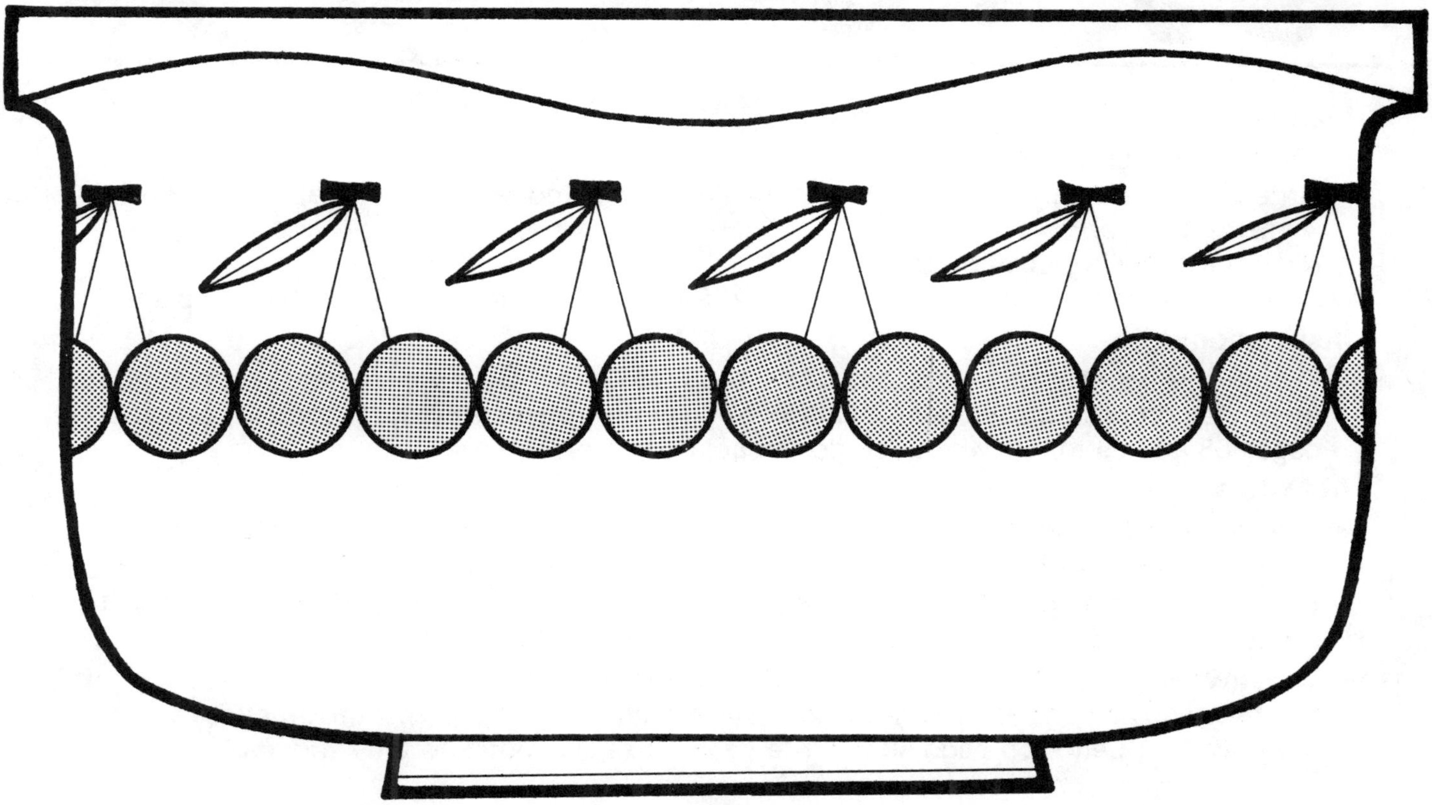

LOVE BUGS

Materials

white or pale green background
large red paper heart with facial features, black arms and legs, and white gloves and boots
red letters spelling **Love Bugs**
sturdy white contruction paper or tagboard for copies of the love bug pattern on page 67

Instructions

Put up the background. Add the letters and large heart. By means of the photocopy or thermofax process, make copies of the love bug pattern on page 67 and the activity sheets on pages 68 and 69 to use when you do the activities described below.

Activities

- **Love Bugs**—Help children create their own love bugs using the pattern on page 67.
- **Buggy Projects**—Plan a trip to the library or bring needed reference materials into the classroom so that your children can do the research needed to complete the science activity sheet on page 68. Allow time for them to share their completed projects.
- **Letter Writing Lesson**—Talk about the parts of a letter and the differences between correct business and personal letter format. Then, have children put the lesson into practice by using the Love Bug Letter on page 69 to write Valentine's Day notes to their friends.

Name ______________________________

LOVE BUG PATTERN

Color this love bug. Then, cut it out and add it to the **Love Bugs** bulletin board.

Name ______________________

DON'T LET INSECTS BUG YOU!

An **insect** is an animal. In its adult stage, an insect has three body parts called the **head**, the **thorax**, and the **abdomen**. An adult insect also has three pairs of legs and two pairs of wings.

Choose an insect to draw and color in the box below. Correctly label its **head**, **thorax**, and **abdomen**. Write the name of the insect on the line at the bottom of the box.

____

In this space, record some facts about your insect.

____

____

____

____

____

____

____

____

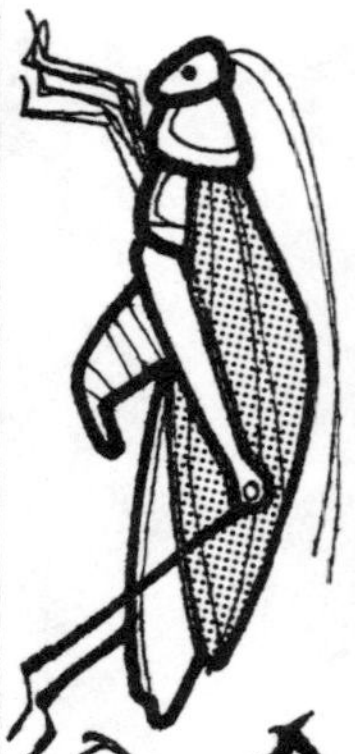

Some Helpful Insects

Some Harmful Insects

A person who studies insects is called an **ENTOMOLOGIST.**

Possible Projects
(Complete at least one.)

1. Read a book or an article about insects.
2. Start an insect collection.
3. Construct a model of your insect and label the body parts.
4. Go to an area, such as an undeveloped field or your own backyard, where you are likely to see various types of insects and take notes on the different ones that you observe.

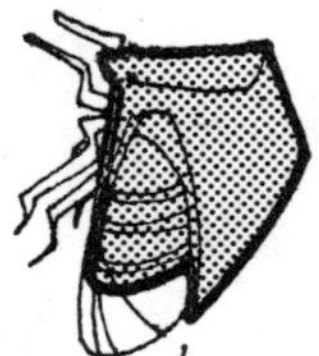

Name ____________________

LOVE BUG LETTER

Use the love bug below to write a Valentine's Day note to one of your friends. After you have finished writing, cut out the bug, fold it in half, and hand deliver your note.

EAT YOUR HEART OUT

Materials

pale green background
large paper mouth with white teeth and red lips
red letters spelling **Eat Your Heart Out**
red or pink construction paper for copies of the pop-up heart pattern on page 71
white construction paper for copies of the mouth and tab patterns on page 72

Instructions

Put up the background. Add the mouth and letters. Using the pattern on page 71, make a large red or pink heart. Cut a bite out of it and staple it to the board near the mouth. By means of the photocopy or thermofax process, make copies of the pop-up heart pattern and instructions on pages 71 and 72 and of the activity sheets on pages 73 and 74 to use when you do the activities described below.

Activities

- **Pop-up Hearts**—Help students assemble Valentine's Day Cards following the instructions and using the pattern pieces on pages 71 and 72.
- **February Fun**—Allow time for children to complete the activity sheet on page 73.
- **Heart Hunt**—For practice and skill reinforcement, have children complete the multiplication activity sheet on page 74. If your students have not yet learned to multiply, substitute suitable addition or subtraction problems before you make copies of the sheet.

Name ____________________

POP-UP HEART PATTERN

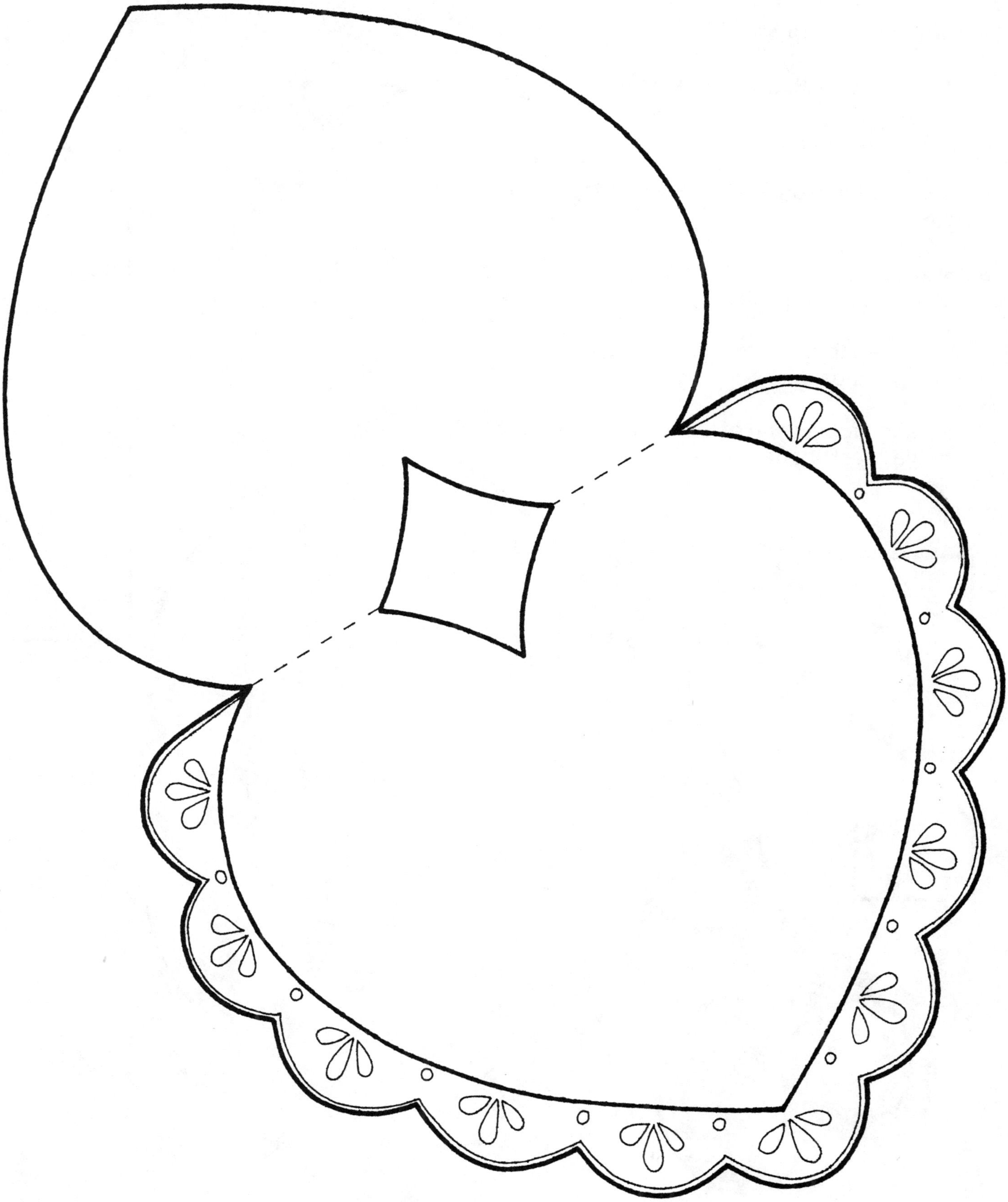

Name ______________________________

POP-UP HEART PATTERN

1. Carefully cut out the paper heart on page 71.
2. Color the mouth on this page.
3. Cut out the mouth and tab.
4. Fold the tab in half along the dotted center line.
5. Fold one tab end up and one tab end down along the dotted lines.
6. Glue the mouth onto the tab slightly above the folded center.
7. Glue one folded end of the tab to each side of the flat heart pattern as shown.

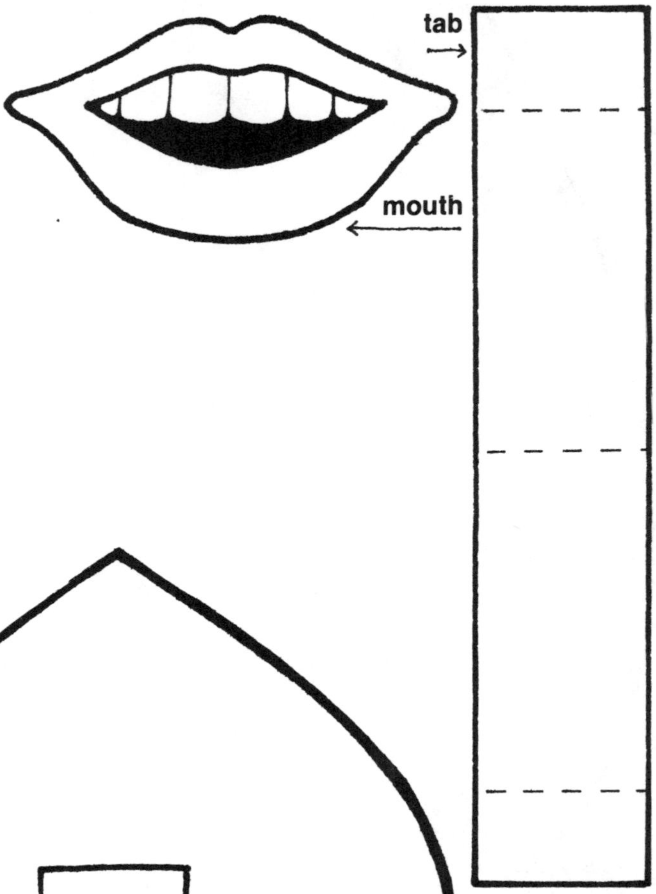

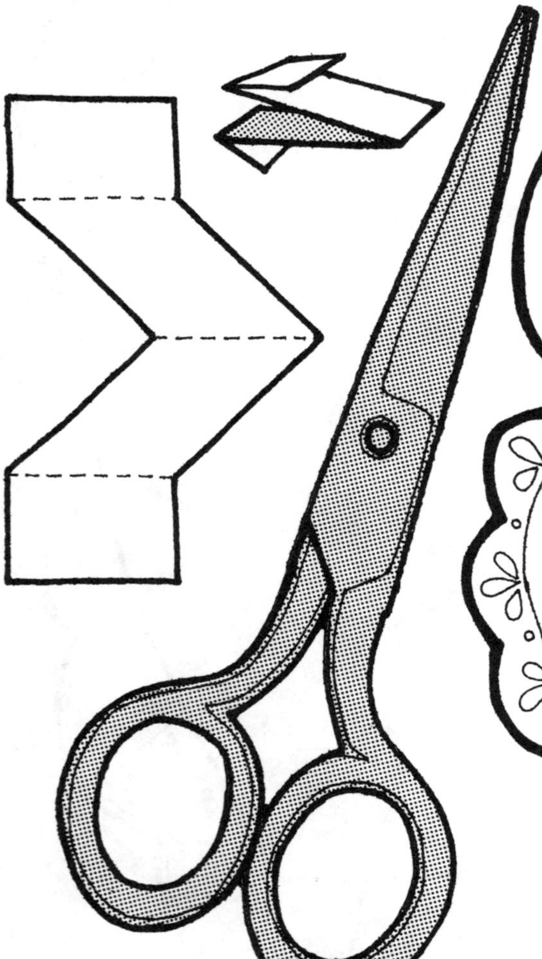

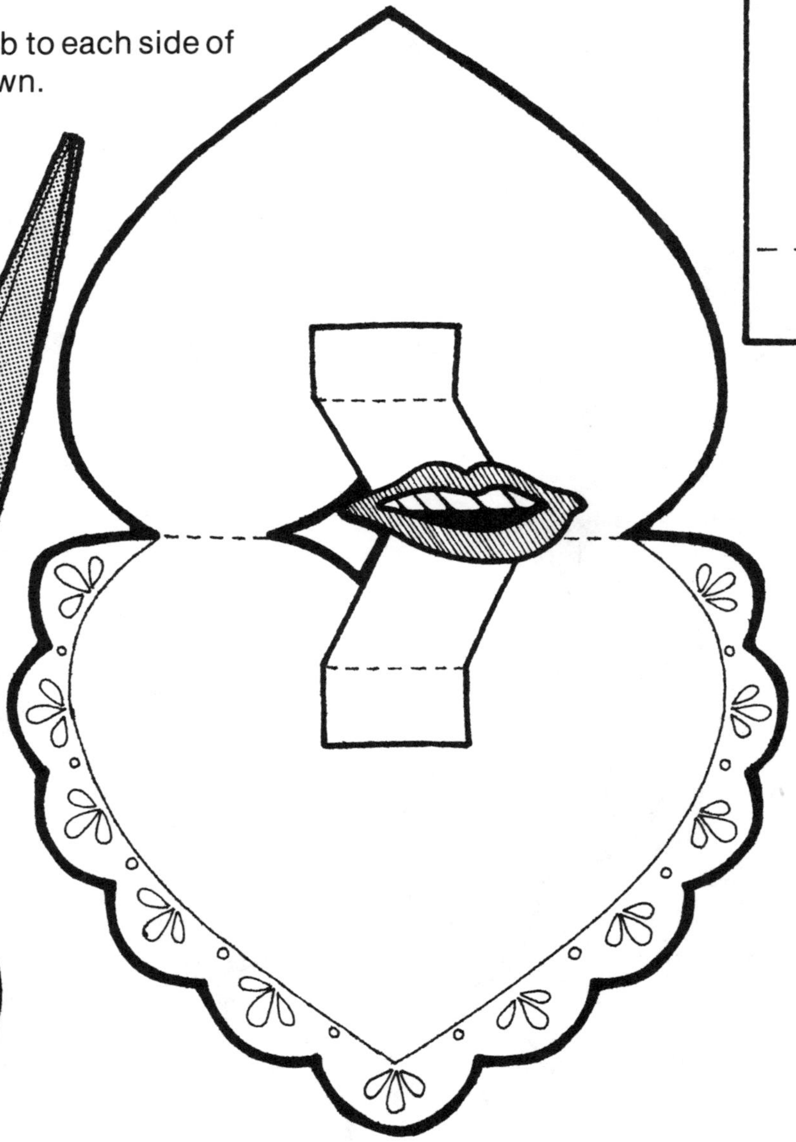

Name ____________________

FEBRUARY FUN

The names of seven of my friends are:

1. ____________________
2. ____________________
3. ____________________
4. ____________________
5. ____________________
6. ____________________
7. ____________________

Seven adjectives to describe my friends are:

1. ____________________
2. ____________________
3. ____________________
4. ____________________
5. ____________________
6. ____________________
7. ____________________

Tongue Twisters

Silly Sam sold Sharon seven slippery seals.

Tiny Twila tried to tie two tricky toddlers to trees.

Aunt Anna asked Aaron about Arnold's ants.

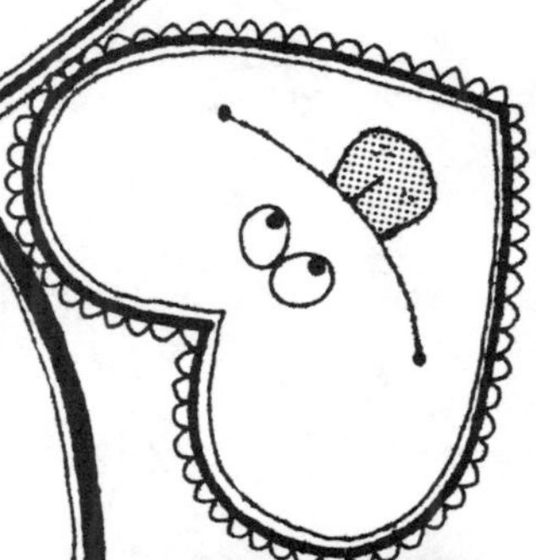

February is the month of President George Washington's and President Abraham Lincoln's birthdays. On the lines below, write a short paragraph telling what you would do if you were elected president of the United States.

How many words can you make from the letters in the word VALENTINE?

1. ____________________
2. ____________________
3. ____________________
4. ____________________
5. ____________________
6. ____________________
7. ____________________
8. ____________________
9. ____________________
10. ____________________
11. ____________________
12. ____________________

Name ______________________

HEART HUNT

Solve each of the multiplication problems in the hearts below. If the last digit of the answer is

9, color the heart white.
8, color the heart blue.
7, color the heart brown.
6, color the heart purple.
5, color the heart orange.
4, color the heart green.
3, color the heart yellow.
2, color the heart red.

1. 522 x8
2. 546 x2
3. 752 x4
4. 642 x3
5. 765 x5
6. 497 x4
7. 821 x3
8. 709 x3
9. 623 x3
10. 237 x4
11. 384 x6
12. 903 x5
13. 246 x4

PATRICK'S POTATO PATCH

Materials

yellow or white background
green letters spelling **Patrick's Potato Patch**
white construction paper for potato people
brown or black construction paper cut in 1-by-8-inch strips for arms and 1-by-12-inch strips for legs
green construction paper for shamrocks

Instructions

Put up the background and add the letters. Using the photocopy or thermofax process, make copies of the potato people pattern on pages 76 and 77, the shamrock pattern on page 78, and the writing activity sheet on page 79 to use in doing the activities described below. Add finished potato people and shamrocks to the board.

Activities

- **Potato People**—Help children color, cut out, and assemble potato people using the pattern pieces and instructions on pages 76 and 77. Add accordion-folded strips of construction paper for arms and legs.
- **Shamrocks**—Have children paint or color copies of the shamrock on page 78 green or let them use this shape as a pattern to follow in cutting shamrocks from green construction paper.
- **Shamrock Stories**—Following both a review of basic grammar and punctuation principles and an explanation of various creative writing techniques, have students select a title from among those suggested on page 79, write original stories, proofread their work, and copy their final drafts on shamrock story sheets. Suggest students cut out their finished shamrock stories and add them to Patrick's Potato Patch.

Name ______________________

POTATO PERSON PATTERN

1. Color and cut out the mouth, eyes, hat, gloves, and shoes on page 77.
2. Color and cut out the potato on this page.
3. Glue the hat, eyes, and mouth to the potato.
4. Accordion fold two 1-by-8-inch strips of construction paper for arms.
5. Accordion fold two 1-by-12-inch strips of construction paper for legs.
6. Glue one glove to one end of each arm.
7. Glue one shoe to one end of each leg.
8. Glue legs and arms to potato as shown.

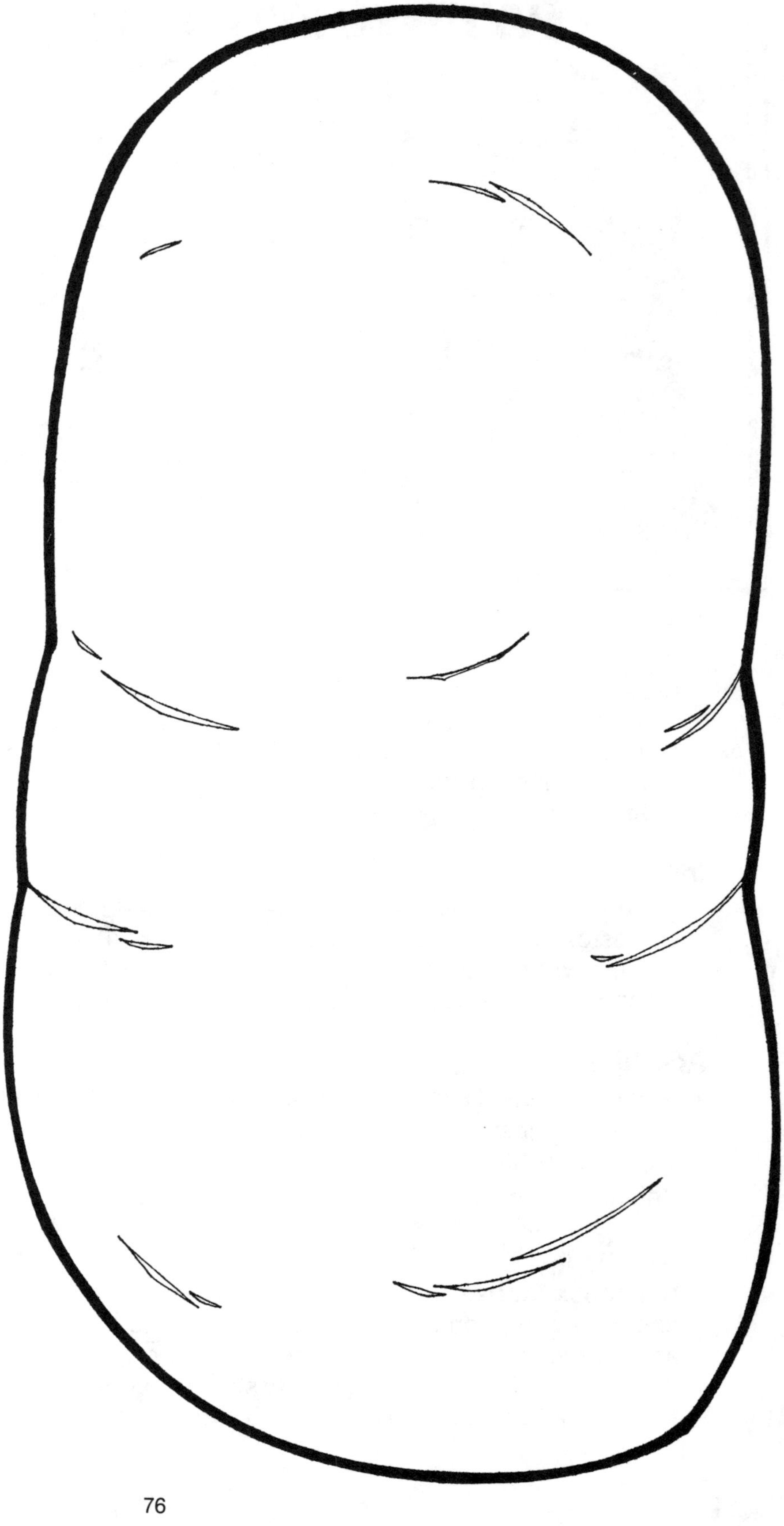

Name ______________________

POTATO PERSON PATTERN

Name ____________________

SHAMROCK PATTERN

Name ____________________

SHAMROCK STORY SHEET

Either select one of the titles below to develop into a story, or use an idea of your own. Write your story on a separate sheet of paper. When you have finished writing, proofread your written work carefully. Then, copy your corrected story in the shamrock below.

Suggested Titles

- The Lucky Little Leprechaun
- A Day in the Life of a Potato
- The Mysterious Man in Green

BEE-WARE! IT'S SPRING

Materials

pale blue background
large yellow-brown beehive
brown letters spelling **Bee-ware! It's Spring**
construction paper in bright colors for flowers
one small paper cup for each child
white or yellow construction paper for bees

Instructions

Put up the background, Add letters, hive, and flowers. Using the photocopy or thermofax process, make copies of the bee pattern on page 81 and the punctuation activity sheet on page 82 to use when you do the activities described below.

Activities

- **Bees**—Help students assemble paper cup honeybees following the instructions and using the pattern pieces on page 81. Suggest children add their finished artwork to the Bee-ware board.
- **Punctuation Activity Sheet**—Complement the bee art lesson with the Bee-ware! activity sheet on page 82.

Name ____________________

BEE PATTERN

1. Color and cut out the bee head, body, and wings.

2. Glue the head to the flat bottom of a small cup.

3. Align the striped body so that the blunt end is nearest the top of the bee's head.

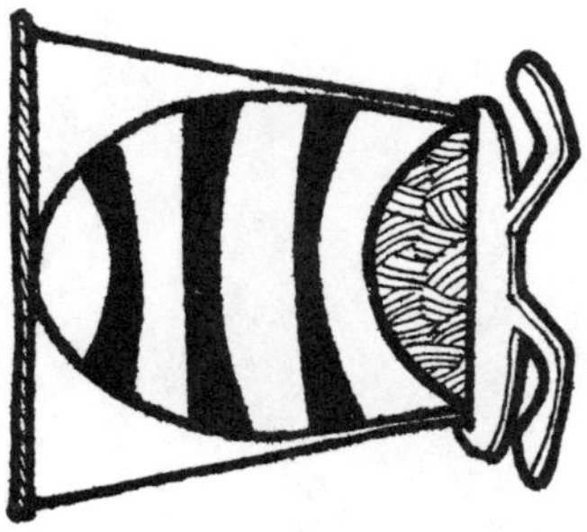

4. Fold wings along dotted lines.

5. Carefully spread glue only on the wing tabs.

6. Attach one wing to each side of the bee's body.

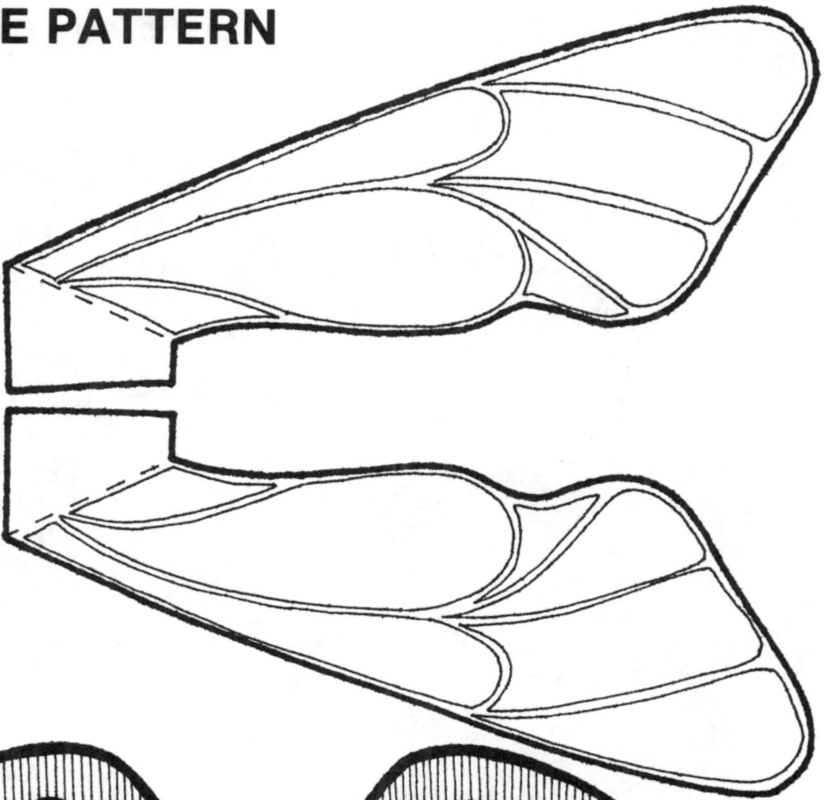

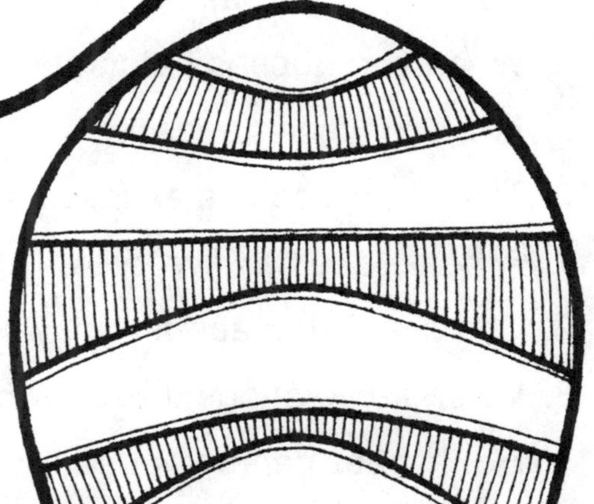

Name ____________________

BEE-WARE!

Correctly punctuate the sentences below.

1. A colony of bees has from 60 000 to 80 000 workers
2. Why does a bee sting
3. Bees fly at a rate of about twelve miles per hour
4. Honeybees live in a colony which is a large group of bees
5. Bees are the only insects that produce food for people to eat
6. Every colony has a queen some workers and some drones
7. Usually a hive has only one queen
8. When two queens hatch at the same time they fight until one of them dies
9. Is a honeybee an insect
10. The honeybee like all insects has a head a thorax and an abdomen
11. A honeybee has five eyes
12. The bee s stomach a honey stomach is used to carry pollen
13. When a bee stings it uses twenty-two muscles
14. Honeybees can detect sour sweet bitter and salty tastes
15. The queen s only job is to lay eggs

MARCH — IN LIKE A LION, OUT LIKE A LAMB

Materials

blue background
pink letters spelling **March, In like a . . .**, and **Out like a . . .**
orange, yellow, brown, white, black, and red construction paper for lions
white, pink, black, and red construction paper for lambs
sheet cotton or cotton balls for fluff on lambs' heads
plastic eyes with movable pupils found in many craft stores *(optional)*

Instructions

Put up the background and add letters. Using the photocopy or thermofax process, make copies of the lamb pattern on pages 84 and 85, the lion pattern on pages 86 and 87, and the alphabetizing activity sheet on page 88. Hand one to each member of your class as you prepare to do the activities described below.

Activities

- **Lambs**—Help children assemble lambs using the pattern pieces and following the instructions on pages 84 and 85. Separate pieces may be cut from white, pink, and black construction paper or entire pattern may be copied on white construction or other sturdy paper and colored.
- **Lions**—Help children assemble lions using the pattern pieces and following the instructions on pages 86 and 87. Separate pieces may be cut from orange, yellow, brown, and black construction paper or entire pattern may be copied on white construction or other sturdy paper and colored.
- **Alphabetizing Animals**—Reinforce your students' alphabetizing skills with this activity sheet, found on page 88.

Name ______________________

LAMB PATTERN

1. Use the shapes on pages 84 and 85 as patterns for pieces to be cut separately from white, pink, black, and red construction paper or copy these pages on white construction or other sturdy paper and color all of the pieces.

   Whether cutting from colored paper or coloring, use pink for the face; white for the fluff, eyes, and ears; black for the nose and facial markings; and red for the tongue.

2. Cut out all of the pieces. If you plan to use plastic eyes, discard the paper ones.

3. Color the pupils of the eyes black. Draw the nose and mouth on the lamb's face.

4. Glue the eyes and ears to the face in the areas marked by dotted lines.

5. Glue cotton to the lamb's fluff, and glue fluff to lamb's face.

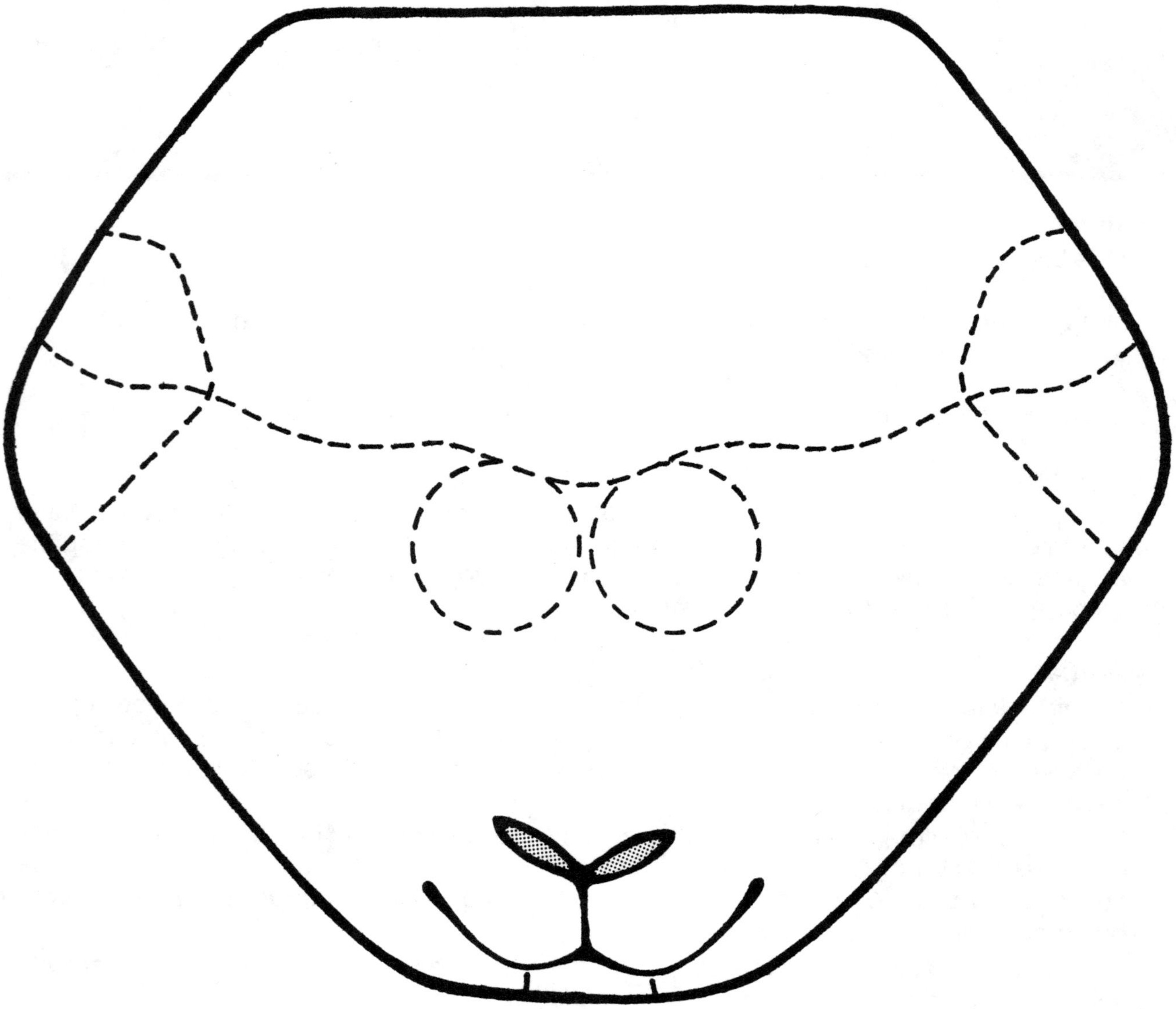

Name ______________________

LAMB PATTERN

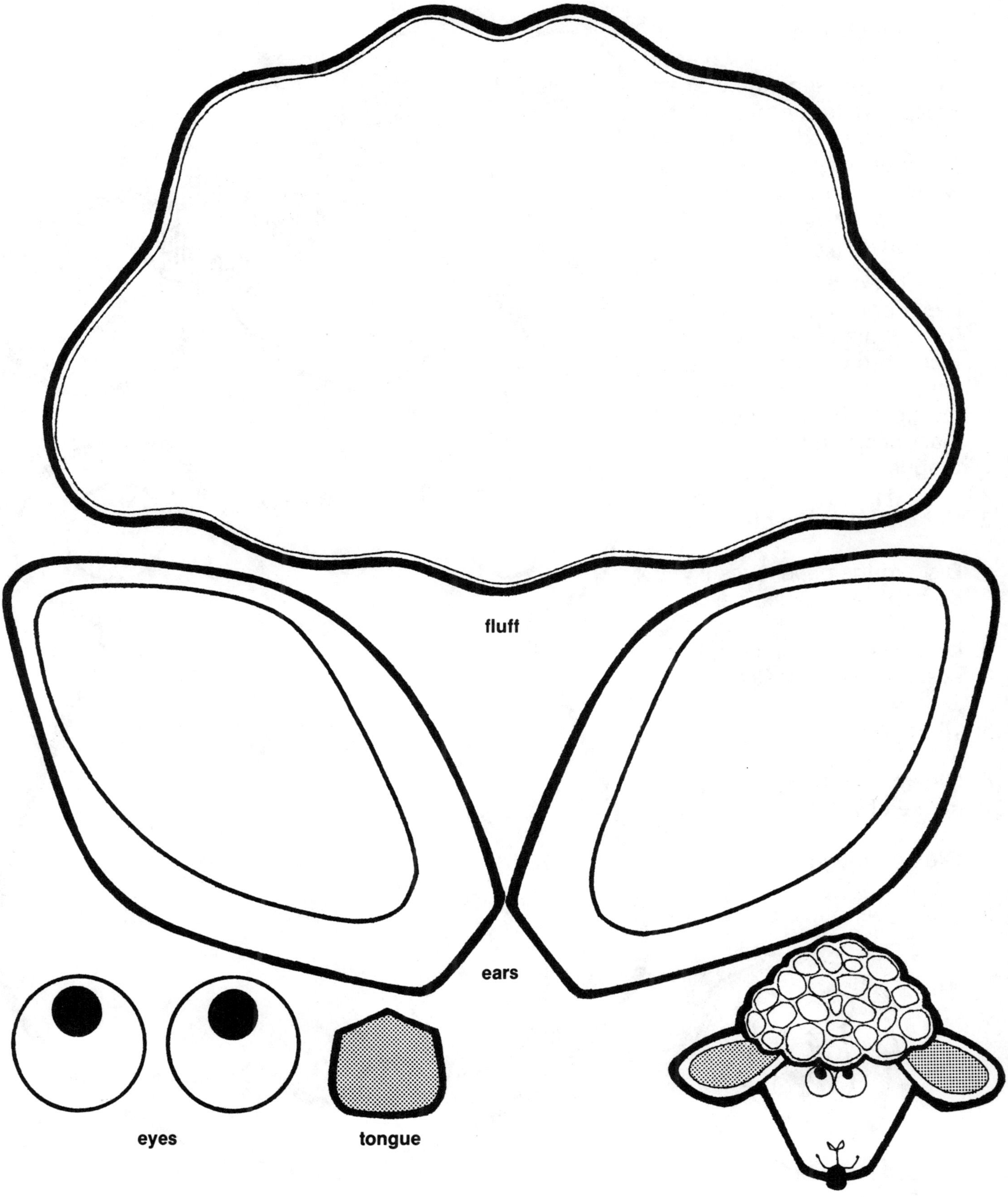

Name ____________________

LION PATTERN

1. Use the shapes on pages 86 and 87 as patterns for pieces to be cut separately from orange, yellow, brown, white, black, and red construction paper or copy these pages on white construction or other sturdy paper and color all of the pieces.

   Whether cutting from colored paper or coloring, use orange for the mane, yellow for the face, brown for the nose, white for the eyes, black for the tip of the nose and facial markings, and red for the tongue.

2. Cut out all of the pieces.
3. Discard the paper eyes if you plan to use plastic ones.
4. Draw markings on face, fill in eyes, and color nose tip black.
5. Glue eyes to face.
6. Glue nose to face in the area marked by dotted lines.
7. Glue on tongue.
8. Glue face to mane.

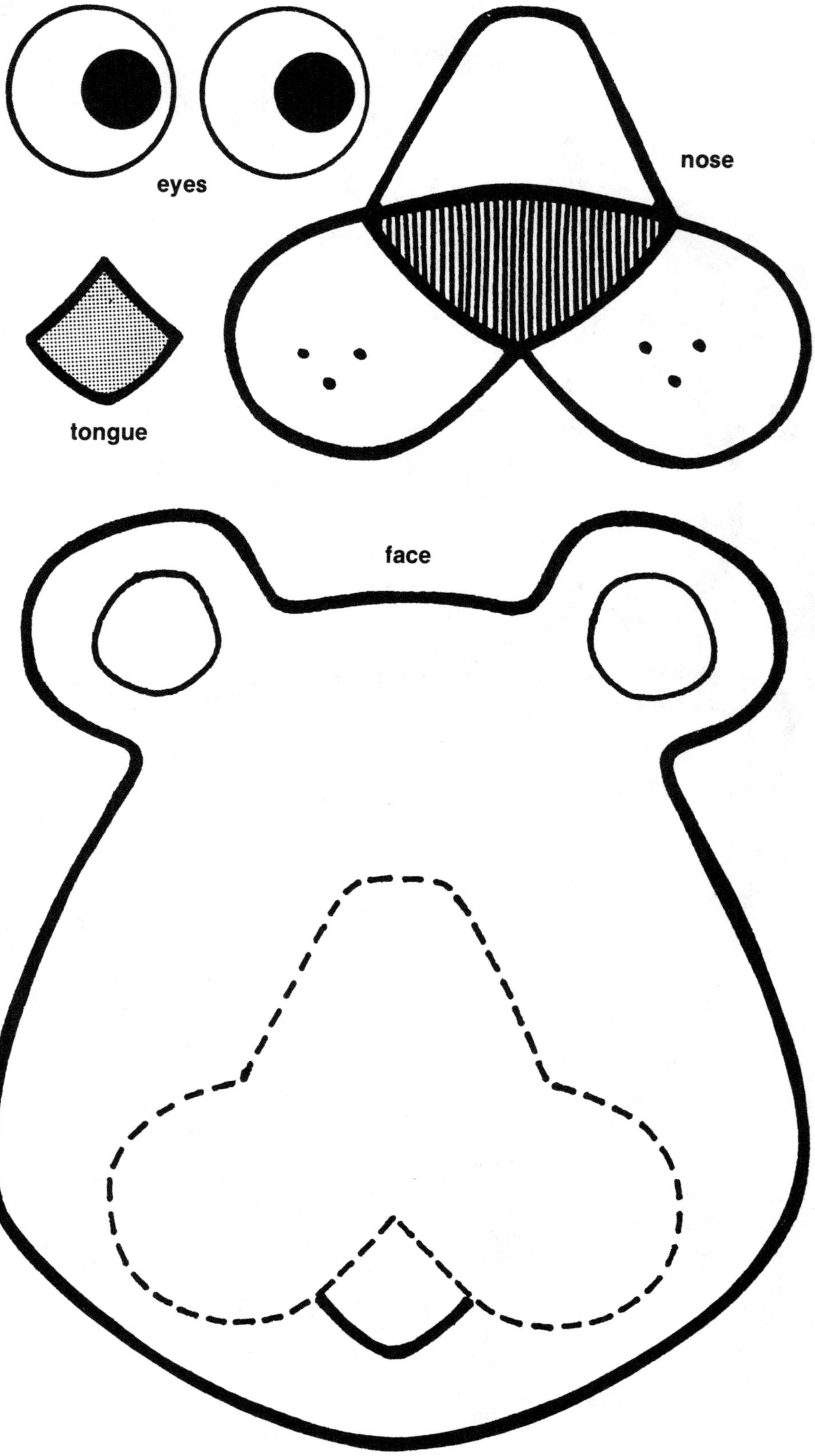

Name ______________________________

LION PATTERN

Name ______________________

ALPHABETIZING ANIMALS

Alphabetize these words by writing a **1** on the line next to the word that comes first, a **2** on the line next to the word that comes second, and so on through **5** for each list.

____ ape
____ aardvark
____ ant
____ alligator
____ armadillo

____ beetle
____ boa
____ bear
____ bison
____ baboon

____ cougar
____ crocodile
____ crow
____ cheetah
____ cat

____ dinosaur
____ duck
____ dog
____ deer
____ dolphin

____ earthworm
____ eel
____ eagle
____ elephant
____ elk

____ frog
____ fox
____ fly
____ fish
____ flea

APRIL TWEETS

Materials

pale blue background
brown letters spelling **April Tweets**
brown butcher paper tree trunk and branches textured with darker brown or black ink or paint
green construction paper for leaves
at least one uncooked egg for each child
darning needle or other similar sharp object for making holes in eggs
cups or bowls to hold blown egg whites and yolks
assorted, bright-colored dyes for eggshells
real, bright-colored feathers (available at craft stores and hobby shops)
yellow, orange, and white construction paper for birds' eyes, feet, and beaks

Instructions

Put up background. Add tree, letters, and leaves. By means of the photocopy or thermofax process, make copies of the bird pattern and instructions on page 90 and of the spelling activity sheet on page 91 to use when doing the activities described below.

Activities

- **Birds**—Help children assemble birds following the instructions and using the pattern pieces on page 90. If they are quite young, you may need to blow their eggs for them or send home instructions and suggest that each child bring an empty (already blown) eggshell from home.
- **April Fools' Test**—The activity sheet on page 91 asks children to correct the misspelling of fifteen spring words.

Name ______________________________

BIRD PATTERN

1. Make a small hole in one end of your egg with a darning needle.
2. Make a slightly larger hole in the opposite end of your egg.
3. Hold your egg over a cup or bowl and blow through the smaller hole until all of the white and yolk come out the larger hole.
4. Allow the empty eggshell to dry.
5. Immerse the empty shell in bright-colored dye.
6. Remove the colored shell and allow it to dry completely.
7. Color the eyes, beak, and feet shapes on this page or use them as patterns for drawing similar shapes on colored construction paper.
8. Cut out all four shapes.
9. Fold top and bottom parts of beak up along dotted lines.
10. Carefully glue eyes, beak, and feet to eggshell.
11. Complete your bird by gluing on real feathers to suggest a crest, wings, and tail.

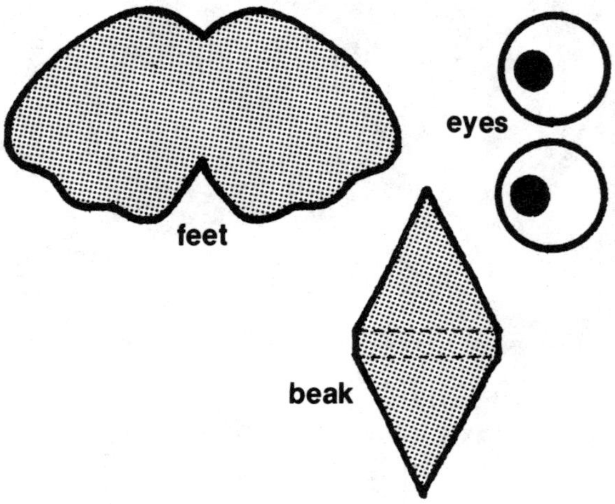

Name ______________________

APRIL FOOLS' TEST

Correct each of the fifteen misspelled words below by writing the correct form of the word on the line next to it.

1. April Fouls Day ______________________
2. bassball ______________________
3. rabitt ______________________
4. twolips ______________________
5. sprng ______________________
6. dafudil ______________________
7. robbun ______________________
8. sonshine ______________________
9. hideing ______________________
10. gardenning ______________________
11. Eastar ______________________
12. jelly beens ______________________
13. tennis shoos ______________________
14. flowrs ______________________
15. choclate ______________________

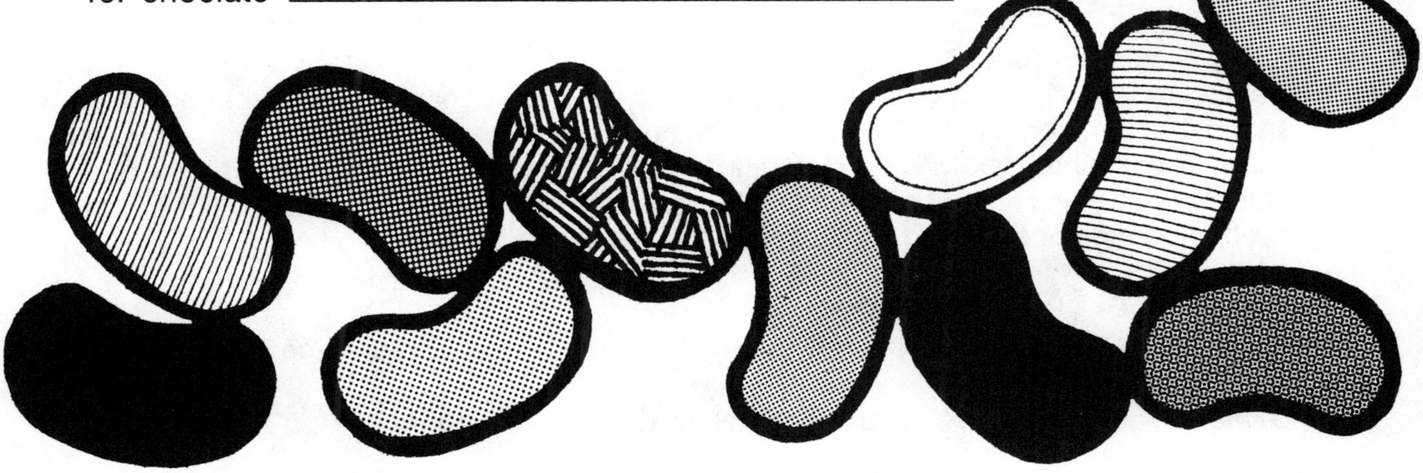

ANNOUNCING THE EGG FACTORY!

Materials

yellow background
large white egg machine with various controls, gauges, lights, knobs, and openings all drawn with a black felt-tipped marking pen or cut from sturdy paper
bright-colored paper for egg entry ramp and wheels
white construction paper for small, plain eggs entering machine
black paper for pipe from which finished eggs tumble
dark purple letters spelling **Announcing the Egg Factory**
white construction paper for copies of egg patterns on pages 94-96
various colors of construction paper for mosaics (Scraps may be used.)

Instructions

Put up the background. Add the machine, ramp, wheels, and pipe. Attach letters and small, plain eggs. By means of the photocopy or thermofax process, make copies of the egg pattern and instructions on pages 93-96 and the game sheet on page 97 to use when you do the activities described below. Have students color these game sheets and then turn them into more durable game boards by mounting them on stiffer paper and laminating them. You will need to provide one die and four markers for use with each board.

Activities

- **Eggs**—Help children create mosaic eggs following the instructions on page 93 and using the patterns on pages 94-96.
- **Game**—Suggest children run an Egg Race (page 97) in their free time.

EGG MOSAIC INSTRUCTIONS

1. Make enough copies of the egg patterns on pages 94, 95, and 96 for each child in your class to have at least one.

2. Hand out the patterns and tell the children to decide what colors they want to use in each outlined area on their eggs.

3. Have children outline their eggs with a black felt-tipped marking pen and then, cut them out.

4. Have each child glue his egg to an egg-shaped backing of stiff construction paper or tagboard.

5. While glue dries, demonstrate both how to tear small pieces of construction paper carefully and how to arrange and glue them neatly on the egg to create an attractive mosaic. Be sure children understand that they should cover their eggs completely with small pieces of paper and not leave any white areas.

6. Make available glue and construction paper in a variety of colors and allow children to create their own mosaics.

7. Display children's finished artwork on the Egg Factory bulletin board.

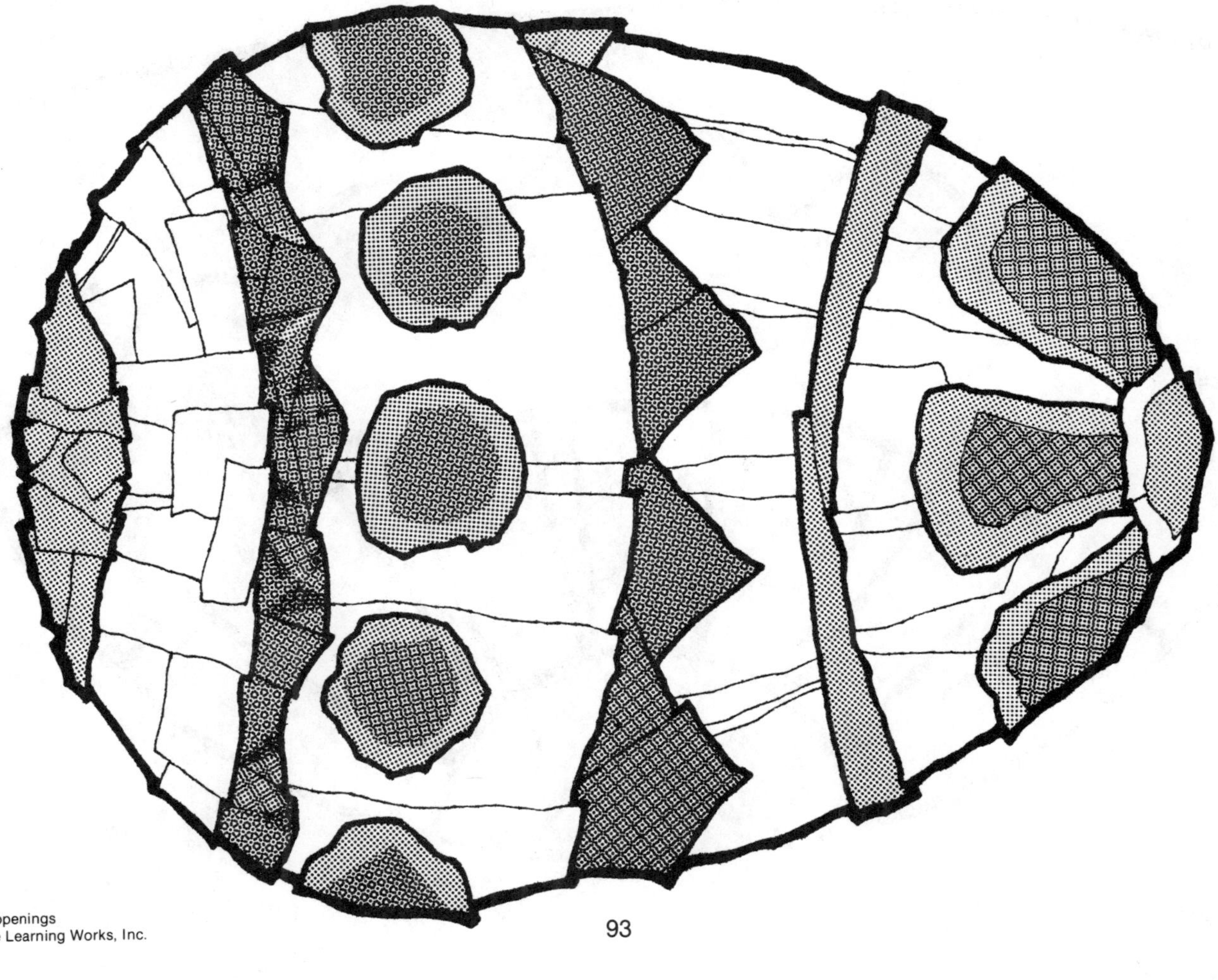

Name ____________________

EGG PATTERN 1

Name ______________________________

EGG PATTERN 2

Name ______________________________

EGG PATTERN 3

Name ______________________________

EGG RACE
2 to 4 Players

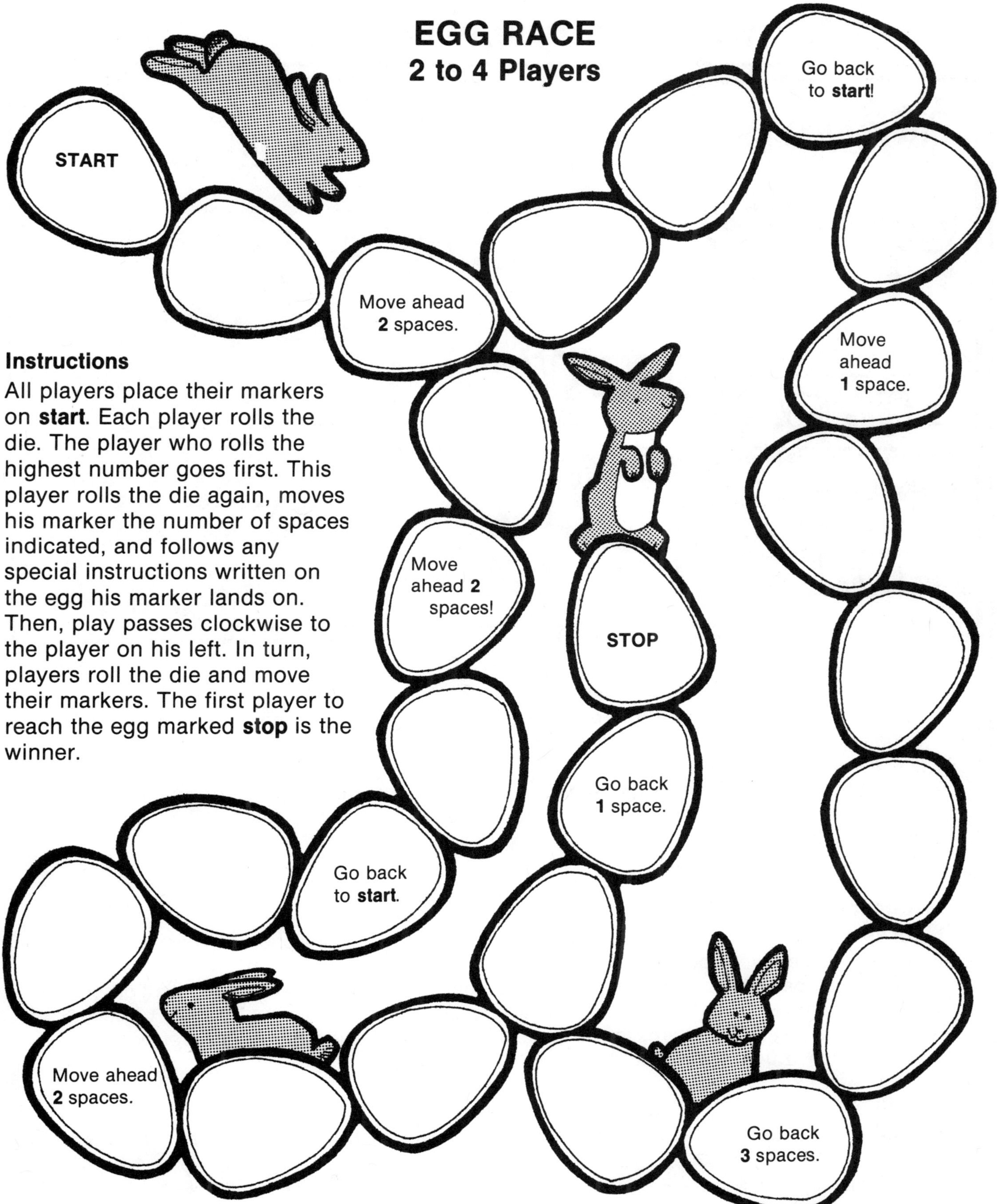

Instructions

All players place their markers on **start**. Each player rolls the die. The player who rolls the highest number goes first. This player rolls the die again, moves his marker the number of spaces indicated, and follows any special instructions written on the egg his marker lands on. Then, play passes clockwise to the player on his left. In turn, players roll the die and move their markers. The first player to reach the egg marked **stop** is the winner.

WORM YOUR WAY INTO APRIL!

Materials

light blue background with dark blue, brown, or black texturing
dark blue letters spelling **Worm Your Way into April!**
large yellow paper bird with red or orange beak and black-and-white eyes
tagboard or other stiff paper for durable copies of the leg and link patterns on page 99
bright-colored construction paper for chain worms to be made by students
white or light-colored paper for worms' heads
black paper for worms' legs

Instructions

Put up the background. Add letters and large yellow bird. Using the photocopy or thermofax process, make several copies of the worm pattern and instructions on page 99. Cut out the leg and link patterns. Lay them on a piece of tagboard, draw around each, and cut out the resulting tagboard shapes. Glue the thin paper copies to the custom-cut tagboard backings to make more durable patterns for student use. Copy the addition activity sheet on page 100 to use when you do the activity described below.

Activities

- **Worms**—Help children cut out and assemble chain worms using the pattern and following the instructions on page 99.
- **Addition Activity Sheet**—For practice and skill reinforcement, have children add the numbers on the Add-'em-Up Worms (page 100).

Name ____________________

WORM PATTERN

1. Using the link pattern, draw and cut out nine links.
2. Carefully glue the two ends of one link together to make a ring.
3. Run the second link through the first and glue the two ends together.
4. Continue in this manner until you have formed a nine-link chain for the worm's body.
5. Color and cut out the worm's head on this page.
6. Use the leg shapes on this page or stiff paper patterns provided to cut ten legs from black construction paper.
7. Cut out the legs and glue them onto the opposite sides of upright links.
8. Finish your worm by gluing his face onto the front of the first link.

head

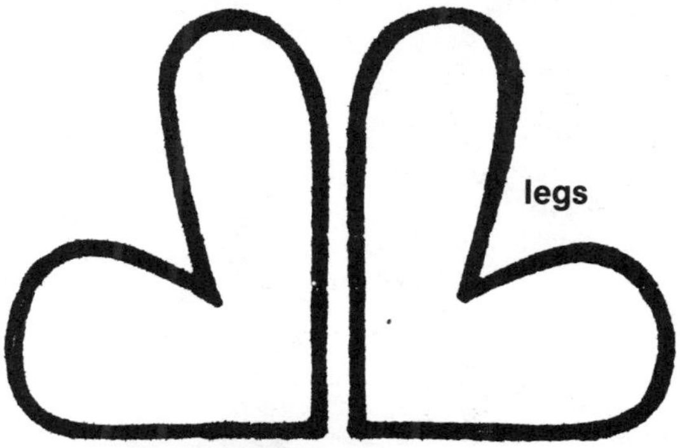

legs

link

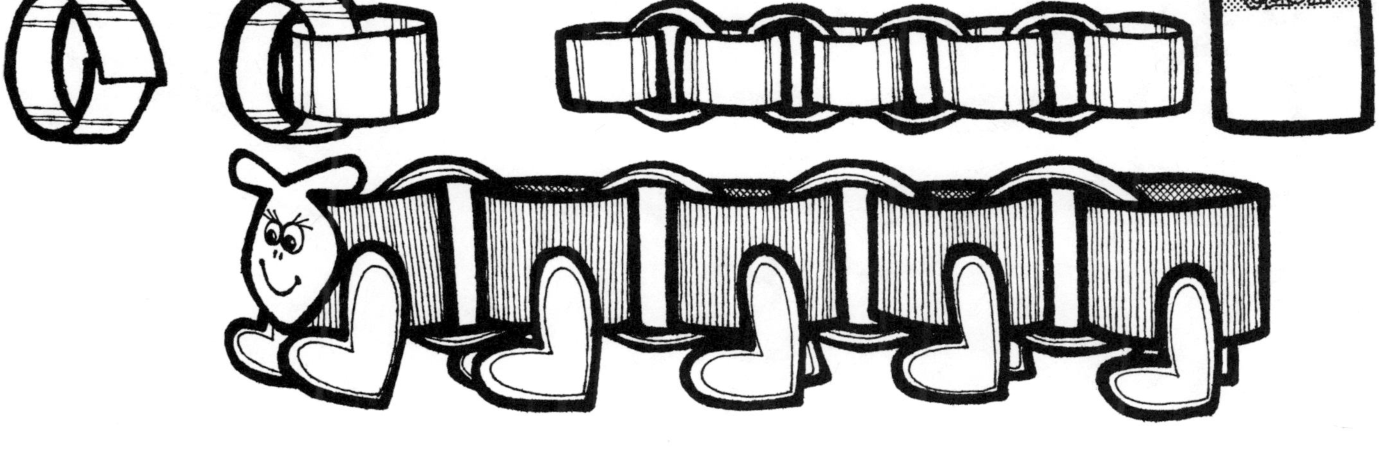

Name ______________________

ADD -'EM-UP WORMS

Add the numbers on each worm. Write your answer on the worm's face.

OUR MAY BOUQUET

Materials

light blue background
very large yellow-brown paper basket with handle
dark blue letters spelling **Our May Bouquet**
tagboard or other stiff paper for durable copies of the daisy center, petal, and leaf patterns on page 102
white construction paper for daisy petals
yellow construction paper for daisy centers
yellow facial tissues for pompon daisy centers
green construction paper for daisy leaves
light-colored thread to tie around gathered tissue
yarn or ribbon to bind Mother's Day cards

Instructions

Put up background. Add basket and letters. Using the photocopy or thermofax process, make several copies of the daisy pattern and instructions on page 102. Cut out the center, petal, and leaf patterns. Lay them on a piece of tagboard, draw around each, and cut out the resulting tagboard shapes. Glue the thin paper copies to the custom-cut tagboard backings to make more durable patterns for student use. Make copies of the Mother's Day card on pages 103-104 to use when you do the activity described below.

Activities

- **Daisies**—Help children cut out and assemble daisies using the pattern and following the instructions on page 102.
- **Mother's Day Card**—Provide each child with a copy of pages 103-104 to color and cut out. Supply small pieces of yarn or ribbon to bind cards.

Name ____________________

DAISY PATTERN

1. Using the petal pattern, draw and cut out eight white daisy petals.

2. Using the center pattern, draw and cut out one yellow daisy center.

3. Crease your daisy petals along the dotted fold line.

4. Glue each daisy petal within one of the marked areas on the daisy center pattern.

5. Using the leaf pattern, draw and cut out four green leaves.

6. Turn your flower over and glue the leaves to the center between pairs of petals.

7. To make pompon for daisy center, fold one piece of yellow facial tissue in half lengthwise.

8. Gather the folded tissue lengthwise at the center; tie it with a piece of sturdy, light-colored thread; separate layers, spread, and fluff.

9. Turn the flower back over and glue the fluffed pompon to the paper daisy center to cover the petal ends.

center

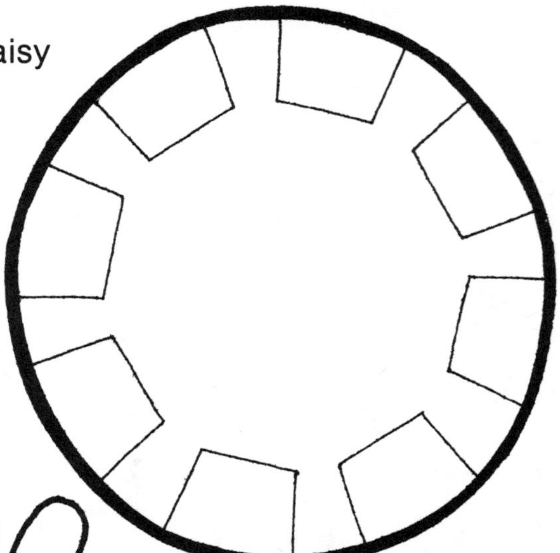

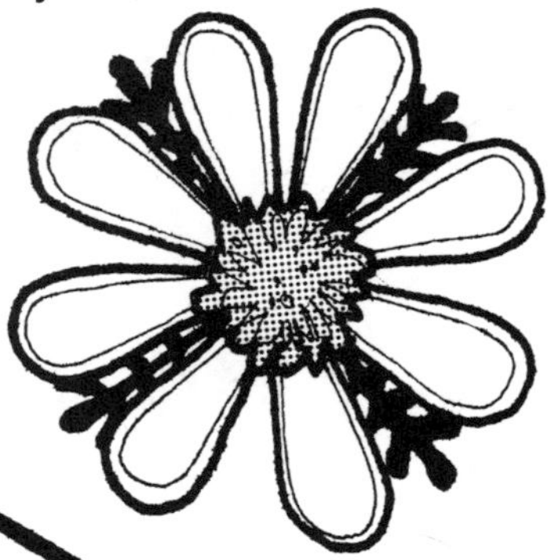

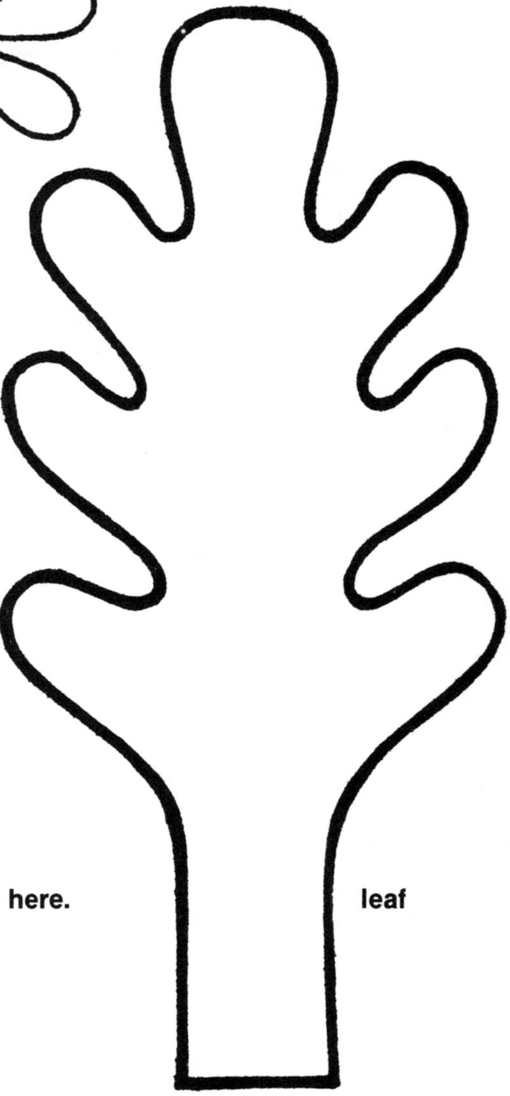

leaf

Fold here.

petal

Name ____________________

MOTHER'S DAY CARD COVER

Color the cover of your Mother's Day card and cut it out. Color and sign the poem page of your card and cut it out. Fold both pages along the dotted fold line. Place the poem page inside the card cover exactly as you wish it to be in the finished card. Punch two evenly spaced holes along the folded edge. To hold the poem page inside the cover, put a small piece of yarn or ribbon through the holes and tie the ends.

May

Name ______________________

MOTHER'S DAY CARD POEM PAGE

When flowers bloom
And skies are clear
And baby robins softly sing,
I think of you
Both night and day
And thank you, Mom,

for everything!

THE BUTTERFLY

Materials

yellow background
black letters spelling **Over fields of buttercups . . . the pretty butterfly!**
tongue depressors for butterflies
construction paper for butterflies

Instructions

Put up the background. Add letters. Using the photocopy or thermofax process, make copies of the butterfly pattern on page 106 on various colors of paper or use white paper and suggest that children do the coloring themselves with felt-tipped marking pens or crayons.

Activities

- **Butterflies**—Help children cut out and assemble their own butterflies using the pattern and following the instructions on page 106.
- **Poetry Activity Sheet**—Use the information and haiku on page 107 to introduce your students to this Japanese poetry form. Then, suggest that students compose and illustrate original haiku.

Name ______________________

BUTTERFLY PATTERN

1. Color butterfly wings.
2. Cut out wings and antennae.
3. Glue wings to one side of tongue depressor.
4. Glue antennae to same side of tongue depressor.
5. Add facial features to other side of tongue depressor with a felt-tipped pen.

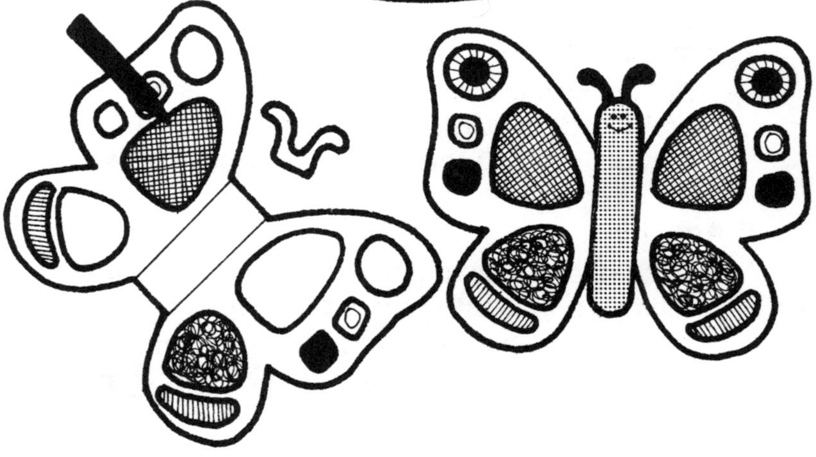

HAIKU

Haiku is a form of Japanese poetry. A haiku is an unrhymed poem consisting of three lines written in a 5-7-5 syllabic pattern and usually referring to nature as it expresses itself in a particular season.

Write several of either the haiku below or your original haiku on the chalkboard for children to read. Review the concept of syllables with your students and explain the 5-7-5 haiku syllabic pattern to them. Then, have students write and illustrate their own haiku.

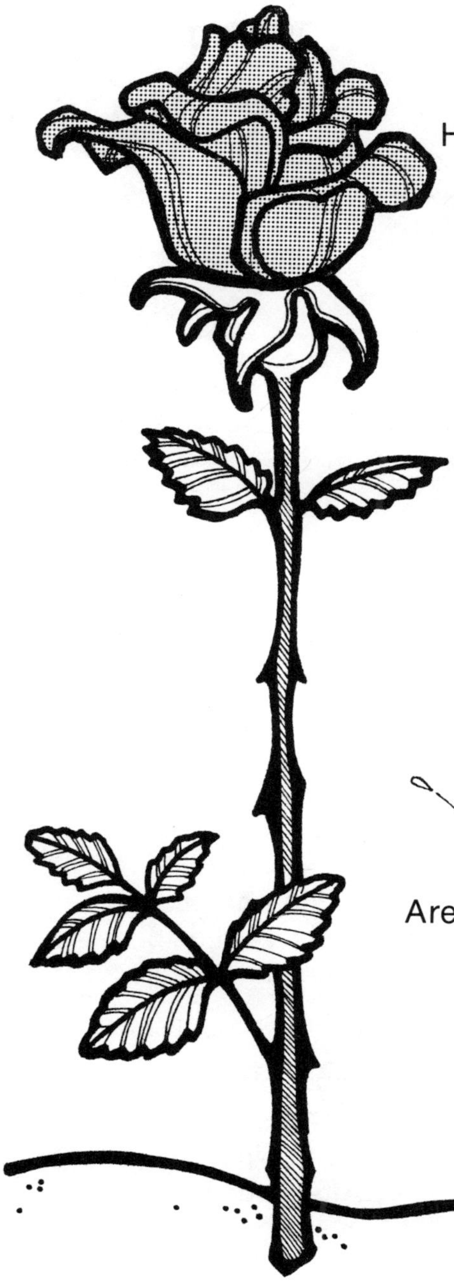

The scent of roses
Hangs heavy on the hot air
Awaiting a breeze.

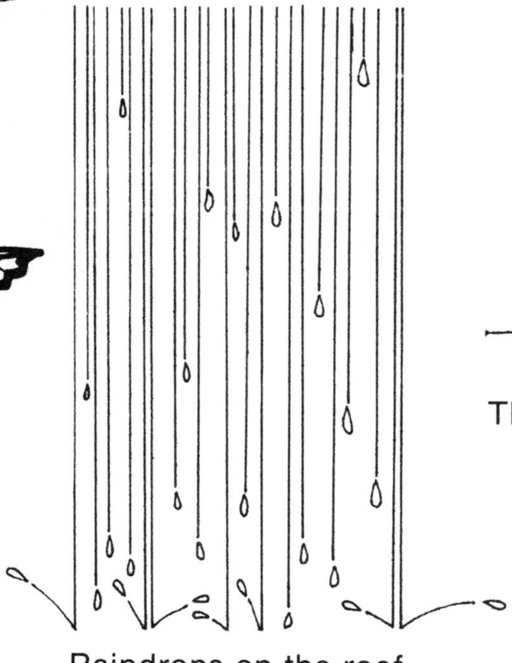

Raindrops on the roof
Are the rhythm of springtime—
Gentle song of life.

Once clothed in scarlet
The tree now stretches naked
Branches toward the sky.

The promise of spring
Sleeps 'neath a blanket of snow
Until the thaw comes.

MOVIN' ON DOWN THE ROAD

Materials

yellow background with brown texturing to suggest ground
green letters spelling **Movin' on Down the Road**
white construction paper or tagboard sign saying **Turtle Race**
brown paper or a lightweight stick or dowel for the signpost
red or orange construction paper for the flowers
green construction paper for leaves
light green paper plates for turtles
white or green paper for copies of the turtle's head, feet, and tail on page 109

Instructions

Put up the background. Add letters, sign, flowers, and leaves. Using the photocopy or thermofax process, make copies of the turtle pattern on page 109 and the booklet on pages 110 and 111 to use when you do the activities described below.

Activities

- **Turtles**—Help children cut out and assemble their own turtles using paper plates and the pattern and instructions on page 109. Enter finished turtles in the turtle race.
- **Story Booklet**—Allow time for children to read, illustrate, and assemble the booklet on pages 110-111 based on Aesop's fable about the tortoise and the hare. After students have completed their booklets, suggest that they add them to the bulletin board. You may also want students to write and illustrate additional booklets based either on other fables by Aesop or on their original stories.

Name ____________________

TURTLE PATTERN

1. Color and cut out the turtle's head, feet, and tail.
2. Fold your paper plate exactly in half with the right side showing.
3. Cut along the fold, creating two identical, semicircular plate halves.
4. On the **wrong** side of one of the plate halves, position your turtle's head, feet, and tail so that the dotted inner tab lines lie along the edge of the plate and the **right** sides of the head, feet, and tail face up.
5. Glue head, feet, and tail in place.
6. Glue the other plate half to the first, **wrong** sides together, so that head, foot, and tail tabs are covered.

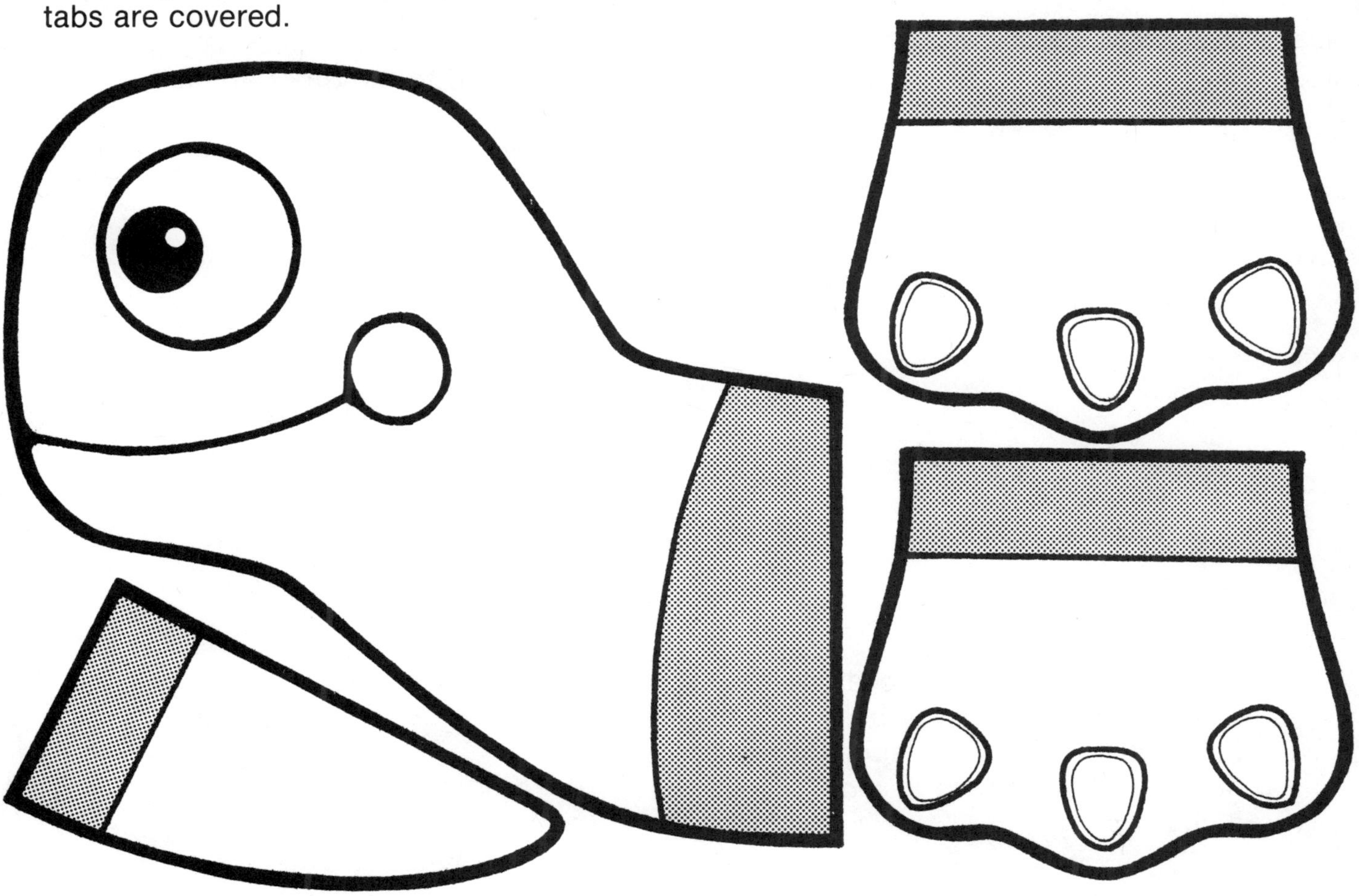

Name ______________________

STORY BOOKLET

Illustrate each of the story pages. Then, cut along the dotted lines to create eight individual pages (one cover and seven numbered pages).

The Tortoise and The Hare

Once the hare was boasting of his speed to the other animals.

1

"I have never yet been beaten when I have put forth my best effort and run at my top speed. I challenge anyone here to race against me."

2

The tortoise said quietly, "I accept your challenge."

3

Name ______________________________

STORY BOOKLET

To assemble your book, stack the pages in numerical order and place the cover on top. Then, staple along the left-hand edge or punch holes and tie with ribbon or yarn.

"What a good joke!" exclaimed the hare. "I could dance 'round you all the way."

"Boast until you've beaten me," responded the tortoise. "Shall we race?"

4

So a course was fixed, and the race began.

Immediately, the hare darted off almost out of sight; but soon he stopped and, in an obvious display of his contempt for the tortoise, lay down to take a nap.

5

The tortoise plodded steadily on and on. When the hare awoke from his nap, he saw the tortoise nearing the finish line and could not catch up in time to save the race.

6

The victorious tortoise declared, "Steady plodding wins the race."

7

Answer Key

Page 19, Who's Wise?
1. 12 2. 12 3. 48 4. 27 5. 37 6. 22 7. 48 8. 39 9. 49 10. 18 11. 65 12. 179 13. 664 14. 469 15. 50 16. 409 17. 256 18. 769 19. 3,736 20. 1,379 21. 4,847 22. 1,789

Page 24, Witch Weigh/Which Way?
1. I, by 2. witch, not 3. Our, bee 4. won, two 5. blue, high 6. We, waste 7. bear, wee 8. see, hare, fowl 9. Beat, flour 10. stake, dew 11. meet, meat 12. pour, ate 13. You're, pale 14. fair, bear 15. It's, stare

Page 31, Gobbler's Inn Menu
Fruits and Vegetables: cranberry sauce, mashed potatoes, corn, green beans
Breads and Cereals: dressing, hot rolls
Meat and Protein: roast turkey, turkey gravy
Milk and Dairy Products: milk, butter
Other Foods: tea, coffee, pumpkin pie

Page 35, Raven's Rhymes. Answers may vary.
1. seen 2. fright 3. said 4. go 5. draw 6. small 7. pies 8. seen 9. die *or* cry 10. eight 11. back 12. you

Page 38, Flag Facts
1. Our flag is sometimes called the "Stars and Stripes."
2. Our flag stands for the American people, their land, and their government.
3. There have been many flags representing our country.
4. The American flag that we use today is red, white, and blue.
5. The stripes on the flag represent the thirteen original colonies.
6. The stars represent our fifty states.
7. We show that we are patriotic when we salute the flag.
8. Usually, we display the flag only in fair weather.
9. Your hand should be placed over your heart when you salute the flag.
10. When someone famous dies, our flag is often flown at half-mast.
11. At school, we say the "Pledge of Allegiance."
12. Our flag was first flown on the moon in 1969 by Neil Armstrong and Edwin Aldrin.
13. A flag should be raised quickly and lowered slowly.
14. A color-bearer is a person who carries the flag.
15. When a flag is worn-out, it should be burned.

Page 46, Attention: Angels

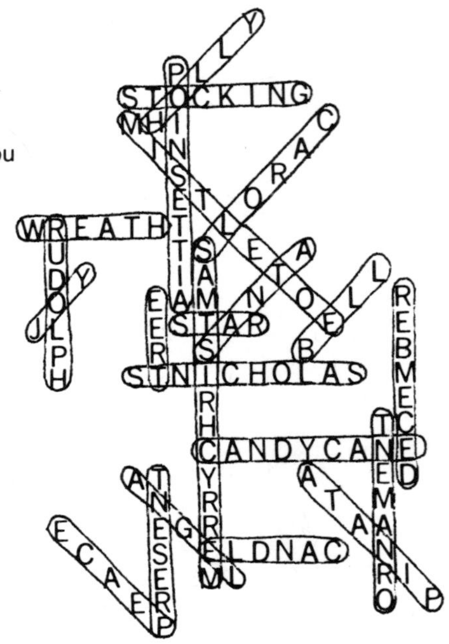

Page 41, Shining Sentences
1. I bought gifts for Bob, Ted, and Ann.
2. Have you seen my coat?
3. How cute that puppy is!
4. Come in here and sit by the fire.
5. The snow is just beautiful!
6. Is winter your favorite season?
7. We went ice skating with Rob, Debbie, and Sue.
8. What is the temperature?
9. Tomorrow will be the first day of Hanukkah.

Page 55, Wintertime
1. January is the first month.
2. I made a resolution.
3. New Year's Day is Jan. 1.
4. It is pretty when it snows.
5. Winter is my favorite season.
6. The roads get very icy.
7. On bad days, there is no school.
8. New Year's Day is a winter holiday.
9. Sometimes we skate on the pond.
10. My friends and I like to ride on sleds.

Page 58, Catch a Sum!
1. 620 2. 1,171 3. 908 4. 671 5. 1,110 6. 752 7. 1,142 8. 902 9. 1,190 10. 1,128 11. 1,248 12. 1,250

Page 65, A Bowl of Cherries
1. 513 2. 183 3. 182 4. 288 5. 157 6. 823 7. 249 8. 179 9. 204 10. 219 11. 389 12. 272 13. 78 14. 189 15. 142 16. 289 17. 530 18. 107

Page 74, Heart Hunt
1. 4,176 2. 1,092 3. 3,008 4. 1,926 5. 3,825 6. 1,988 7. 2,463 8. 2,127 9. 1,869 10. 948 11. 2,304 12. 4,515 13. 984

Page 82, Bee-ware!
1. A colony of bees has from 60,000 to 80,000 workers.
2. Why does a bee sting?
3. Bees fly at a rate of about twelve miles per hour.
4. Honeybees live in a colony, which is a large group of bees.
5. Bees are the only insects that produce food for people to eat.
6. Every colony has a queen, some workers, and some drones.
7. Usually, a hive has only one queen.
8. When two queens hatch at the same time, they fight until one of them dies.
9. Is a honeybee an insect?
10. The honeybee, like all insects, has a head, a thorax, and an abdomen.
11. The honeybee has five eyes.
12. The bee's stomach, a honey stomach, is used to carry pollen.
13. When a bee stings, it uses twenty-two muscles.
14. Honeybees can detect sour, sweet, bitter, and salty tastes.
15. The queen's only job is to lay eggs.

Page 62, Word Families

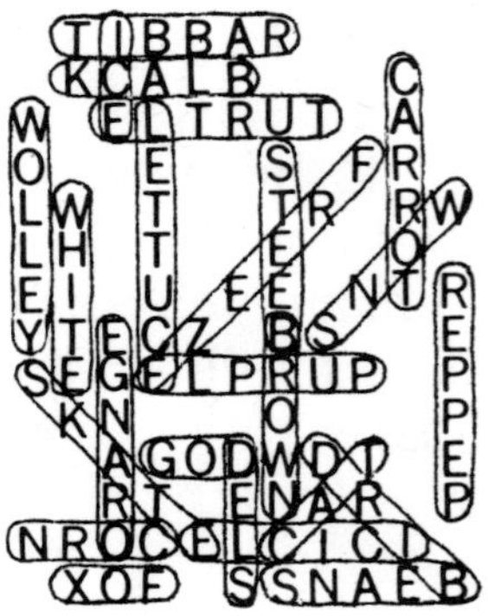

Page 88, Alphabetizing Animals
A. 4, 1, 3, 2, 5 B. 3, 5, 2, 4, 1 C. 3, 4, 5, 2, 1 D. 2, 5, 3, 1, 4 E. 2, 3, 1, 4, 5 F. 5, 4, 3, 1, 2

Page 91, April Fools' Test
1. April Fools' Day 2. baseball 3. rabbit 4. tulips 5. spring 6. daffodil 7. robin 8. sunshine 9. hiding 10. gardening 11. Easter 12. jelly beans 13. tennis shoes 14. flowers 15. chocolate